Praise for

PEOPLE ARE GOOD...

"*People Are Good* is a must read for those in need of spiritual nourishment. Humanity is beautifully messy, but all too often, it's the messiness that gets all the attention. I'm grateful to *People Are Good* for lending voice to the beauty."

—Lisa Fisher, author of the award-winning and best-selling *Admissions by Design*

"Why is it that human beings always tend to focus on the 10 percent of what's wrong in the world and overlook the 90 percent of what's great? *People Are Good* draws our attention back to the fundamental truth that there is much goodness and light in the hearts of so many. Anna McHargue tells us about a few of these amazing people. Their stories will give you a new basis for optimism, and inspire the best in you as well."

—Mark Traylor, author of *Radicalizing Peace: How Your Good, Small, Faithful Steps Can Change the World*

"We are a people of the word. We love stories. Each of our lives is full of stories just like *People Are Good,* which is replete with stories of what we encounter in our otherwise ordinary lives. These stories, however, remind us of what Dorothy Day called the holiness of the ordinary, that each moment is sacred. Read this fine work, and join in the celebration of stories."

—Dr. Steve Shaw, author of *The Presidents and Their Faith*

"With so many ways to gain information, it's easy to get inundated with discouraging events and tragedies. *People Are Good* is a gentle reminder that most of humankind is good-hearted and generous of spirit. The short stories are the perfect serving size for this balm to my world-weary soul."

—Cara Grandle, author, teacher, and encourager on Periscope@caragrandle and founder of author4TheAuthor

"It seems that no matter where you turn, darkness prevails. And that feeling can make you feel totally overwhelmed at the most unusual times . . . until you begin to realize that there are good people in the world doing really great things. *People Are Good* exists to remind you every time you pick it up that the world can be a kind place. From story to story, I was blessed to read what others are doing to change the lives of the people around them . . . because people are good."

—Stacey Stone, WGTS 91.9 Afternoon Show Co-Host in Washington D.C., and author of *The Rescued Breed: When Jesus Shows Up and Transforms Your Pack*

"When life has you discouraged, the smallest act of kindness can change your whole day. *People Are Good* is an entire collection of these moments, sharing how ordinary people have touched the lives of others with the simplest acts of kindness."

—Kattarin Kirk, graciousstumble.blogspot.com

"Uplifting! *People Are Good* inspires and showcases the goodness inside others. Acts of kindness from both strangers and friends can turn around a situation and leave a lasting memory. These heartfelt stories from people highlighting the generosity of others are sure to delight."

—Stephannie Hughes, author

"In a world filled with chaos and catastrophes, it becomes easy to see only strife and disappointment. *People Are Good* is a breath of fresh air, a wonderful reminder that there is an essential goodness inside us all. These simple acts of kindness displayed by ordinary people from all walks of life will surely restore your faith in humanity."

—Brandi O'Brien, author and periodical blogger,
antiquatedbride.wordpress.com

"With her collection of real stories, Anna McHargue has offered a refreshing break from the daily grind. It's nice to crack a smile, shed a tear, and feel human. Anna has given us a way to engage with others we've never met. I will keep a copy for myself and keep another on hand as a gift for friends."

—Darryl B. Womack, author of *Tales of Westerford*

"Anna McHargue beautifully highlights humanity at its best in these simple, yet poignant stories of kindness and selflessness. *People Are Good* is an effortless read which can be enjoyed in small doses, one story at a time, to make the moments last. It is also the kind of book that is hard to put down, as each story begs for the next one."

—Laetitia Mizero Hellerud, intercultural competency develop-
ment consultant and author of *Being at Home in the World:*
Cross-Cultural Leadership Lessons to Guide Your Journey

"*People Are Good* by Anna McHargue is truly a must read for people of all ages and in every stage of life. Not only will the stories make you laugh, cry, encourage you and give you hope, they also will change you for the better. *People Are Good* will motivate you to want to be that person who helps someone in small ways that have a huge impact. Reading this book has inspired me to pay more attention to moments in time, previously unnoticed in my busyness, to grab opportunities to do something good for another."

—Susan Vitalis, M.D., author of *Still Listening:*
How to Hear God's Direction at Life's Crossroads

PEOPLE ARE GOOD

100 True Stories to Restore Your Faith in Humanity

ANNAMARIE MCHARGUE

People Are Good: *100 True Stories to Restore Your Faith in Humanity*
AnnaMarie McHargue © 2017

Print ISBN: 978-1-61206-149-8
eBook ISBN: 978-1-61206-150-4

Cover Design: Leslie Hertling
Interior Layout & Design: Fusion Creative Works, FusionCW.com
Editor: Anita Stephens

For more information, visit PeopleAreGoodCommunity.com or
WordsWithSisters.com.

To purchase this book at highly discounted prices,
go to AlohaPublishing.com or email alohapublishing@gmail.com.

Published by

ALOHA
PUBLISHING

AlohaPublishing.com
Printed in the United States of America

To LOUIS RUNFOLA, our beloved Papa,
whose goodness never waivers and
whose love is tremendous.

Author's Note:

The following stories were voluntarily submitted by individuals who wanted to share their experience of how people are good in the world. The author and publisher created this book using the truth as it was expressed from each contributor's point of view.

CONTENTS

People Are Good . . . When Times Feel Uncertain

People Are Good . . . When They Make Others a Priority

People Are Good . . . Even When Parenting Isn't

People Are Good . . . When Reflecting the Face of Jesus

People Are Good . . . In Frightful Weather

INTRODUCTION

None of us is perfect. I get it. We fail. We fight. We hold grudges. We marinate in bitterness. We talk about others.

But haven't you had enough of all that? I certainly have. Let's make some changes. Let's work together to turn this around, to bask in the small successes that keep us afloat each day, the small acts that change our perspective or give us hope.

People Are Good is just that—a collection of true stories told by real people who have something wonderful to share. We all know someone who has changed our life in some way, big or small. We all have seen people acting in kindness or love. We all know how much better it feels to stir the good than to spill the bad.

Many of the names in these 100 stories have been changed as some prefer to keep their benefactor anonymous, letting their acts speak for themselves. Others prefer to announce the names loudly and strongly in celebration of a life changed. Either way, these stories are meant to remind us that we are surrounded by goodness and that our small acts can make a meaningful difference in the friends, family—and strangers—we see each day.

PEOPLE ARE GOOD...

Even When Our Health Isn't

Weston

When my aunt made the impossibly difficult decision to move across the country at age 84 to be closer to family, we never imagined that six short months later, she would be in the emergency room with a collapsing lung. She was admitted immediately, and after a week of testing and living in the hospital, diagnosed with stage IV lung cancer. There was nothing to be done but wait.

The nurses came and went, some with better bedside manner than others. All of them were capable and kind, most of them women. Then came Weston, a nurse with a bright smile and wavy blond ponytail. He introduced himself, looked over the chart and began the business of checking vitals, just as all the other nurses had done. But after a moment, he stopped and sat down. He picked up my aunt's hand and held it. Then he asked her how she was. It was obvious that she was far from well. She hadn't showered since before her arrival and hadn't had the will to brush her teeth or hair. She looked old. And sick. And broken.

He said that he saw in her chart she was from New York. What had she done there for work? Where did she live? Was there a mister she had left broken-hearted? How did she wind up in Idaho? The more he spoke, the more she engaged. The ease with which they connected was incredible, with him holding her hand all the while. Within moments, she had told him the better part of her story, complete with loves and losses and a touch of scandal. They laughed and she sat up straighter. They understood each other immediately, and by the dim lights and the beeping machines, the most beautiful thing happened between them. He began to flirt with her. He flirted in the kind of charming, old-world way men no longer use when they communicate with women. His intonation changed and he called her by the pet name the love of her life had once used. He had only learned of it moments earlier, when she poured the abridged details of her life into the kindness of his outstretched hand.

Over the course of days, he flirted with her every time he walked into that room, and she looked forward to seeing him. She died two weeks later, in her home, surrounded by family. But in those moments with Weston, she wasn't an old, dying woman who lived with her cats and never married. When he came into her room, she was a woman; a vibrant woman with a story, a woman worthy of affection and the attention of a handsome young nurse. He was the very last man in her life to make her feel like a lady. And for that, I am eternally grateful.

Elise, Boise, Idaho

The Scarf

On a sunny afternoon in August, I had a few free hours after work, so I went to our quaint downtown street to stroll through the local stores. I made my way to a sweet little shop owned by a lovely lady and went in. I started looking around but was distracted by my purpose, not really concentrating on her fine linens and silks. She was unpacking a box of beautiful Italian scarves and asked if I needed help. My eyes, suddenly and unexpectedly, began to well up with tears as I told her I would be losing my hair soon and didn't know what I was going to do with my bald head.

She immediately stood up and hugged me until the tears stopped. She then sat me down in front of a mirror. She unwrapped one of the beautiful scarves, twisted it around my head, and then tied it so that the scarf and beads came down the side of my neck! WOW! This wonderful woman had given me so much more than an answer—she showed me how to do it myself, and then she GAVE me this very expensive scarf! She was exactly what I needed that moment and I will never forget her act of kindness.

Vicki, Novato, California

Undiagnosed

I spent four years wandering aimlessly in a punishing desert called "undiagnosed illness." My body betrayed me. My fears overwhelmed me. Doctors couldn't crack me. One day, I got an infection, which was the straw that broke this camel's back. I began to search the bowels of the internet, looking near and far for someone who could improve my quality of life. Answers were just a luxurious dream; I'd long accepted that a solution would never be afforded to me—until the internet gifted me with a world-renowned genius in another state, who was willing to see me within two months' time.

By my second visit with this internet gem, an 80-year-old doctor had not only given me answers to my sickness, but dignity. My pain—and my story—mattered to him in a deeply personal way they had not before. No matter how many physicians I'd seen, the result was the same: I was a number, a list of symptoms. Here, though, to this doctor, I was a person, experiencing loss, and in need of a resolution to my symptoms.

I temporarily moved to another state in order to undergo rigorous treatments. During this time, the highlight of my week was going to see my new doctor. I pulled strength from his essence, watching his eyes dance as he spoke of his research and all the people it would help. I was getting lost in the vast wells of his kindness. But a dark day had come when a nurse entered an exam room and told me my beloved doctor, whom I'd come to love like a father, was dying of cancer. I couldn't hear the words she spoke next. Instead, I rushed out to hug him and tell him I loved him. Taking my face into his frail, speckled hands, he paused and then said, "It's so good to see you. I love you, too." He chose to see me throughout his dying days, overseeing my treatments, even as he was undergoing his own.

Each time I called, sometimes after hours, to ask a question or to discuss complications, upon recognizing me he would say, "It's so good to hear your voice. Now, tell me, what's going on?" Who was I that he would love me so well? Who was I that he would provide such exceptional care, even as the final grains of sand slipped from his own hourglass? I once sat in his office and thanked him for the gift of time. Not only was he giving me his time, his final years, but also he was giving me my time, my life back. He told me the only thanks necessary was watching the light come back into my eyes as my body began to heal. I never thanked him for restoring my dignity or healing my soul, but he did it because people are good.

Stacey, Clermont, Florida

Annie

On an unseasonably warm day in February 2017, I ambled up the wooden boardwalk to my front door. My mind raced with thoughts, and several emotions vied for my attention as my friend, Annie, who was watching my kids, greeted me at my front door.

"How did the appointment go?" she asked.

Weeks of unusual symptoms led me to that day and a visit with my physician to discuss a diagnosis. I leaned my back onto the cool surface of the kitchen counter while I relayed the details to my friend.

"The doctor said all my symptoms could be stemming from anxiety and depression," I hesitantly told my friend.

The truth was I still was grappling with this idea myself. I had convinced myself only a physical ailment could be causing the shaky hands, racing heart, lack of appetite and sleep deprivation. The next sentence was even harder to get past my lips.

"The doctor prescribed me an anti-depressant." Fear, loneliness and defeat permeated my words. I felt discouraged, anxious and alone.

"Oh, good!" Annie exclaimed.

Her reaction shocked me. I had prepared myself for a pitying look, silence or a quick change of subject. My dear friend proceeded to tell me how counseling and medication helped her through some rough patches in her life. While the internet only shared stories of mental health medicine gone wrong, she painted a positive picture of how much treatment had helped her. More important than her testimony of successful medical care was her openness in sharing her struggles with depression. She made me feel understood and known. Fear and shame slid away as I realized I had friends in this hard place.

Mental health isn't something we talk openly about in our society, leading those living with mental disorders feeling lonely and misunderstood. Annie's courage in sharing her story with me has led me to be open with others about my own challenges. I hope I can be the same encouraging and empowering friend to others that Annie has been to me.

Lindsay, location unknown

New Jersey

For whatever reason, I found myself frightened by the prospect of moving to New Jersey. I had heard the people there were proud and loyal to their own. Would they welcome me, an outsider? Would I fit in? I would be alone in the new city. How would I acclimate? Only one month after my move, I discovered I needed major dental surgery. The previous 11 months of my life had been spent caring for my grandmother in an assisted living facility and taking care of my own health, including my teeth, had been neglected.

My pain was intense and my emotions were a mess. On the day of the surgery, I cried upon waking and upon walking and upon breathing. Everything about that day made me upset and my biggest concern was that I had no car, so I had to rely on someone to drop me off and pick me up. Walking into that office alone was bad enough, but following the surgery I had to sit on a bench in the lobby of the dentist's building to wait on my ride.

That was when an angel in the form of an older New Jersey woman swooped in to care about me, a stranger. She wore a business suit and tightly gripped her briefcase as she blew into the door, headed somewhere important. She saw tears stream down my very swollen face.

"Are you okay?" was the only introduction she gave and when I could not answer, she sat down beside me on the bench.

We established through my garble of gauze that I was waiting for my ride, in pain and currently alone in my wait. She stayed with me, patting my hand until my friend arrived. After opening the door to help me out, she was gone in a flash to the elevators with no chance for me to even ask her name.

From that day forward I stopped allowing any preconceived notions about people to creep into my heart, regardless of where they lived or how I imagined they were supposed to act. We lived in New Jersey for almost nine years, and I opened my heart to some of the most wonderful people because this one woman took the time to sit on a bench and offer comfort to a stranger in distress.

Stacey, Washington, D.C.

The $20 Challenge

We all know life can change in an instant. And when it does, we all hope that we can count on people to be there for us. Sometimes we're disappointed. Sometimes we get what we hope for. And then, sometimes, we get a miracle that restores our faith in the goodness of others.

June 1, 2017 started as an ordinary day. I had a doctor's appointment, and after receiving good news, I decided to treat myself to lunch on the patio of my favorite restaurant.

But on my way there, a teenager on his phone blew through a red light at full speed and in a moment changed my day and my life to anything but ordinary.

Diagnosed with six concussions, a traumatic brain injury and post-concussive syndrome, I eventually lost my full-time career with one of the world's largest high-tech companies and struggled daily to keep up with my life with three very small children. From the outside, I look the same, but neurofatigue, memory loss, aphasia and emotional changes like anxiety and depression are my constant companions. The science behind TBI (traumatic brain injury) is still largely not understood and treatments center around rest. But one day, I was informed of a multi-day experimental therapy at an out-of-state clinic. It was exactly what I'd been looking for.

Unfortunately, because we'd been turned into a one-income household overnight, treatments not covered by insurance were not in the cards. I mentioned on Facebook that I'd found my TBI therapy unicorn . . . too bad I couldn't do it.

But then one friend replied . . . *start a GoFundMe. I'll donate.* Something inside told me to go for it. The goal was lofty—almost $15,000. By the end of the weekend, my friends from Facebook had raised a quarter of the money. Every time my phone dinged with another notification, I felt overwhelmed with what God had in store.

A friend took the link off Facebook and placed it on a message board for alumni of the university where my husband and I graduated. He challenged one-third of the membership—many of whom I'd never met in person—to give $20 each to fund my treatment. One week from my original post, we were more than 50 percent of the way there. Another member then offered to make a sizeable donation to make up whatever was still needed come Monday morning. By Monday though, we had blown through the number. He gave anyway. One week later, we closed out the challenge.

Life can change in an instant. But the instant I want to remember is not the moment a small SUV slammed into my car. It's the 123 instantaneous notices of friends, family and even strangers, who took up a challenge to help me be me again.

Kristen, location unknown

Getting It Right

My pastor likes to say, "I love Christianity. It's Christians I could do without." He's joking (mostly), but he's right. We're humans and humans mess up a lot. But sometimes we get it right. Sandy is a woman who got it right. She has a son who played on the high school football team. Every week, under the Friday night lights, it was all about cheering him and his fellow Panthers on to victory. As the weeks went by though, Sandy began paying more attention to a situation in the stands than to the action on the field. She noticed Cee Cee, a fellow football mom whose health appeared to worsen every week.

Before one particular game at a tailgate party, Sandy felt a persistent push to act. She went straight to Cee Cee—a woman she barely knew—and asked how she could help. What these football moms couldn't possibly have known was that God was drawing up a miraculous play—one that would save a life.

Sandy learned that Cec Cee suffered from primary sclerosing cholangitis (PSC), a chronic disease that leads to liver damage and, eventually, liver failure. Cee Cee was in desperate need of a liver transplant. With no one in her family as a match, Cee Cee could only wait and pray as her name remained on the transplant waiting list. Without hesitation, or knowing what she was getting herself into, Sandy volunteered to be tested.

She was a perfect match. Backed by an entire community's prayers, surgeons removed Cee Cee's nearly useless liver and replaced it with 60 percent of Sandy's healthy one. The results were immediate and miraculous.

Today Cee Cee has another chance at more—more weddings, more graduations, more anniversaries, more life. And all because Sandy refused to remain on the sidelines. That persistent push Sandy was feeling at a pregame party was God telling her there is love in the doing. It's where miracles live.

Curt, Nashville, Tennessee

The Pitching Debut

In 2010, my sweet son, Joey, was diagnosed with Down syndrome at four months old. We walked into the office expecting only some blood work and left with a special needs diagnosis. The weight seemed unbearable, and I suddenly felt very alone, like my family and I were on an island no one else could reach. We began the process of telling those around us: our parents, my brothers, close friends. And slowly, one interaction at a time, the rest of the world. This did not seem like the appropriate time for a Facebook announcement. As I looked into the eyes of our neighbors and friends and shared our heartache, I braced myself for "the wall." I was certain people would begin to distance themselves from us, unsure of how to interact with us now that we were a "special needs family." I imagined people slowly backing away—not right in that moment, but over time, pity creating a chasm between us and our former community.

I couldn't have been more wrong.

In fact, our relationships grew stronger. Some people grieved with us, shedding tears as we wrestled through the doctors' appointments and worries for the future. Others encouraged us to keep putting one foot in front of the other, assuring us good days were still ahead. (And, were they ever right!) We were hugged, prayed for, and cared for at every turn. In the early days, when depression got the best of me, our friends loved us fiercely, offering hugs, bringing meals, coming over to fold laundry and load the dishwasher. When we walked into church, people would stand in line to snuggle our beautiful baby. As time went on, our community became Joey's fan club, monitoring his growth and accomplishments, coming to Down syndrome awareness events and showing up for him and our whole family—time after time.

Joey, who is now 7, recently won the opportunity to throw the first pitch at a minor league baseball game. Our family was gifted 25 tickets to share with family and friends. It seemed like a lot at first. But then we started getting texts and phone calls from people who heard about his "pitching debut" and wanted to join in the fun. I contacted the group sales department to purchase additional seats. And a few weeks later, I called again. And then again. When the big day finally arrived, 125 people cheered as my amazing boy proudly launched a baseball from the pitcher's mound. Thirty seconds, that's how long he was on the field. But every person there was thrilled to be part of the day. On the day Joey was diagnosed, I sat in my living room, staring at a family picture, trying to imagine our future. It seemed sad, overwhelming and lonely. I wish I could go back and tell that girl what a beautiful, joy-filled life we have, thanks, in large part, to the amazing community that has rallied around us.

Katy, Ohio

My Grandpa

In the 1950s when my dad was 7 years old, his 35-year-old dad (my Grandpa Martin) was admitted to the hospital in Great Falls, Montana, where he had 60 percent of his ulcer-riddled stomach removed. During the surgery he lost over 30 pints of blood. He had a very rare blood type and there was not enough blood available in the hospital or in his town. The doctors and the community put out emergency pleas on the radio to all towns in Montana and far into Canada. That day, 30 selfless people answered the call for help, some driving as many as eight hours to donate blood for my Grandpa.

After 200 penicillin shots, 30 pints of blood, lots of prayers and many weeks in the hospital, my grandpa came home alive. In the 60 years that followed, Grandpa Martin enriched the lives of many: my grandma, my dad and uncle, seven grandchildren, many great-grandchildren, his community, his church, and me, his granddaughter. I will never be able to thank those blood donors who couldn't have known that their good deed would afford me the opportunity to enjoy a 30-year friendship with a man I otherwise might never have known.

Kira, Boise, Idaho

Road Warriors

I found myself in the clean and tidy cubical of my doctor's office. The plan was to wait in the white room until my doctor gave me a pain-relieving injection. I was expecting it to go as smoothly as it had in the past, anticipating the joy of a four-hour reprieve. The procedure went as planned until the doctor decided to double the medicine to triple my relief time to 12 hours. A great idea—in theory.

The shot was delivered successfully and the medicine delivered an instant effect. Only it didn't just relieve the normal pain. The medicine ran past the problematic nerve and completely numbed my sciatic nerve in my left leg. One whole leg and half my lower body were completely paralyzed. I couldn't feel a thing. It was like my leg belonged to a stranger. I couldn't bend my knee. I couldn't lift my hip. I couldn't flex my foot, let alone walk or stand. The doctor told me to expect the medicine to last all the way through the full 12 hours. Driving was completely out of the question.

I was stranded.

Before I realized how inconvenienced I was with a dead leg, and even before I articulated a cry for help, my friend and her husband headed my way. They didn't wait for me to voice an appeal. They saw the situation for what it was and made plans to serve me without waiting for me to ask. Their decision was automatic and selfless. They both gave up a day's work. They drove 30 minutes one way only to turn around and drive back. After waiting for the doctor to release me, they supervised me as I wobbled to the car on crutches, unable to move my limp leg out of my own way. They took me home, settled me safely in my own recliner, and even thought to drive my car home for me. I was impressed, blessed and amazed that they were willing to sacrifice their day, the money or contacts they could have each made as self-employed realtors, all to save me.

I want to be that kind of listener, that kind of friend. Ready to read between the lines, jump into action and live selflessly.

Cara, Mulino, Oregon

Smarties

In the fall of 2011, my youngest daughter, at age 8, was diagnosed with type 1 diabetes. Type 1 diabetes is an auto-immune disease that affects only 5 percent (about 29 million people) of the total population of diabetics in the United States. As newbie parents, we had to learn quickly how to take care of our daughter with insulin injections, blood sugar checks, frequent doctor visits, etc. This includes treating an occasional low blood sugar with juice or glucose tablets. Later that spring, our family decided to run a local 5K color run together.

As we gathered at the starting line, our daughter quietly turned to me and said, "Mom, I'm feeling low." We checked her blood sugar and she was 56, nowhere near normal range. She was in need of some sugar to get her up and ready to jog!

Usually, we are so prepared, and even over prepared, but this morning diabetes got the best of us! My husband and I knew that we couldn't let her run a race with a dangerous low, so we would have to sit this one out if we couldn't help her—and fast. Much to our delight, we had run into a new friend of ours whom we met at a diabetes support group. Having had type 1 for several years, she was prepared, and ready to run the race. She handed us a roll of Smarties candies—more than enough to get our daughter up to healthy range just as the race

41

was about to begin. Her quick thinking made a world of difference to our daughter and to our family that day. We could enjoy the race and celebrate a job well done instead of heading home, defeated.

Jessica, Redding, California

Friends and Neighbors

In 2007, I was diagnosed with breast cancer. I am known to be independent and strong willed, so I believed I could manage my treatments while still caring for my three young children. Should things get tough, I thought, I could rely on the help of my husband and parents. Two of my neighbors knew better. Without asking my opinion, they took control and did what I would never ask. They organized meals, picked up my kids when I was at chemo and came to my appointments to take notes because my husband and I were still in a fog. They held my hand and cried with me, which is something I'd normally only do in private. They allowed me to have these moments of weakness and, in doing so, gave me the strength I needed to fight for my health.

Audrey, Boise, Idaho

Best Friend

Whenever I am asked who my best friend is, I don't have to hesitate for a second. My best friend is my older sister. She is the best friend anyone could ever hope for, and she is always there when I need her. To me, that's what a best friend is all about.

For several months I had been feeling frustrated and worthless. My life seemed to be lacking purpose. While I had been dealing with chronic limitations brought on by a number of injuries, I had no idea this was the calm before the storm as I was about to suffer a potentially life-threatening medical event.

As I was lying in my hospital bed, alone physically and emotionally, my sister called. She was the first person in my immediate family I talked with since my hospitalization. What she said pulled me out of my darkness.

She said, "When I heard you had a mini stroke, I became terrified. You have no idea how important you are to me and I can't fathom not having you to support me. I need you."

The words she spoke gave me a reason to fight. I wasn't only leaning on her, but she needed to lean on me as well. Knowing that I mattered gave me the strength I needed to pull myself out of the fog I was in and fight for my life.

Sue, Minnesota

Strawberries

In 2006, my thoughts were focused on waiting for a liver and kidney transplant. I had already been on the transplant list for almost a year, and my body was feeling every second that passed by. The longer a person waits for a lifesaving organ, the more challenging the days become. As days passed, I started to become more discouraged. I didn't want to feel this way—constantly worried that I wouldn't get a second chance at life—so I turned my life back over to the Lord. That day I realized that no matter what happened—transplant or no transplant—I could handle the outcome because His strength was enough.

One weekend in April that year, two friends invited me to a conference in Atlanta, hosted by one of our favorite speakers. I used every bit of energy I had to attend this event, and thankfully it turned out to be a wonderful and memorable occasion. Dinner was included that evening, so we were assigned to a table of about 10 people.

My friends conveyed my life story to those seated at our table that night, and instantly I received numerous questions concerning my experience in the transplant world. I had been on dialysis for about two years, which became a topic of interest we discussed that evening. As a result, I began to share some of the benefits and difficulties of peritoneal dialysis.

Once dialysis entered my life, many changes came with it, such as certain foods being banned from my diet. Chocolate was a favorite treat of mine that I had to say goodbye to. A horrifying thought, my friends said! In many ways, I think they were more upset over this news than learning I was waiting for a transplant! When dessert came, each plate was beautifully decorated with chocolate cake, strawberries and whipped cream. I sat there staring at these delectable treats remembering I could not eat one bite.

One gentleman at our table interrupted my thoughts by asking me if I could eat strawberries. I told him that I could, and within moments, I had a mound of strawberries on a plate in front of me. Each person at the table had given me every single strawberry on his or her plate. I was so elated, blessed and humbled all at once by this small but very big act of kindness toward me, and I have never forgotten their generous behavior. These few individuals, who did not even know me, encouraged me and brightened my world at a time when it was very difficult to find joy. Amazingly, one week after this conference, I received my gift of life.

Heather, LaGrange, Georgia

Packing

Rather than stay in the comfort of the U.S., her home country, Robyn chose to sacrifice more than we can imagine by caring for children in Africa; not just caring, but loving them unconditionally. She provides a home to the homeless, feeds the hungry, clothes the naked. Robyn receives no awards, recognition, acknowledgment or money for her work, and relies on financial gifts from people to partner with so her work can carry on.

Every time I visit her, she graciously opens her home. On my last visit, I had difficulty packing while preparing to fly home, due to a traumatic injury. I was unable to focus and became totally overwhelmed to the point of walking in circles, accomplishing nothing. Time was ticking by and I was nowhere near being ready to leave for my plane. Robyn came into my room, asked how I was doing and became concerned. She could see that I had accomplished very little and was unraveling. With a smile and a hug, she directed me to sit on my bed and proceeded to pack my bags. At that moment, I felt her unconditional love for me and knew everything was going to be okay.

Susan, Battle Lake, Minnesota

$100 Bills

A mother of four was diagnosed with late-stage cancer. She didn't have the money necessary to start her treatment and pay for all the other expenses related to her disease. But friends jumped in. Jesse and Jenna reached out to friends and family and asked them if they could spare $100. If so, they were to bring their contribution to a restaurant downtown at a designated time. Their goal was to get 100 people to give $100.

Under false pretenses, the young mother and her family came to breakfast and were offered a seat. Jesse and Jenna asked if she minded answering a few questions on video to share with others about her sickness. She agreed. Soon after the video began, a line formed outside the restaurant. The number grew to hundreds of people, many of whom they knew, many they did not—but each and every one of them was there to deliver a $100 bill. In addition to the money, these people also shared their love, wishing her well in the hard days to come.

It was a simple act for some in the community and a difficult one for others but either way, the kindness and generosity shown by both friends and strangers made a huge difference for this woman and her family.

Michael, Sunnyvale, California

PEOPLE ARE GOOD...

When Times Feel Uncertain

My Sister

One day, I found myself homeless. Not the horrible I-have-to-live-on-the-streets homeless, but rather someone without a home. The owner of the house I was renting needed to move back in. My son and I very quickly had nowhere to go. As many people have done, I relied on the generosity of family and wound up on my sister's doorstep. She and her husband have three kids and an already full house. But I was greeted with open arms. She cleaned out the storage room where she kept her baking supplies (she is a professional baker) and made me a small area to sleep. I was happy we had landed somewhere safe.

A few weeks later after returning home from work, I went to my spot in the storage area to find more evidence of my sister's love. She had transformed the area into a beautiful bedroom. I had a real bed with lovely bedding. I had lamps and nightstands. As if this weren't enough, her husband reminded me that their home was my home and that we were welcome to stay as long as we wanted. Never before had I felt so loved.

Charissa, Riverside, California

Full Circle

When I saw Drs. Kirk and Kim for the first time after several years, it felt as though no time had passed as we picked up where we left off all those years ago. We had initially met at a time when I was working on a mission project that needed the expertise they could provide, and they were looking for a mission they could do together as a couple. This was truly a God-ordained meeting. We worked on the same project for a few years and then went in different directions, hearing different calls.

During the time of our reuniting, I went to a church service where Kirk, now a trained physician and pastor, was preaching. At the time, I was drifting, not knowing if I had a purpose in life and if I did, I had no clue what it was. I was far from being the person I was when I first met Kirk and Kim, now wandering in the desert of uncertainty. What Kirk said as he introduced me to the congregation turned my world upside down. His words realigned and reframed the way I was looking at my life and provided me a mission—something that had been eluding me for months.

His transforming words were, "One person changed the course of our life. We all may have one person in our life who changes the direction of where our life is headed. When we met Susan, it was clear that God sent her to change the course of our life forever."

His statement opened my eyes and showed me what God was doing in my life. It opened my eyes to see that my purpose was there all along—I just wasn't recognizing it. His words found me. We had come full circle.

Susan, Minnesota

Fleeing

I lived the first five years of my life in Burundi, and those five years created a lifetime of warm, happy memories for me. But I was unaware of most of the country's turmoil. One night I was awakened during the darkest hours, literally and figuratively, and it felt like I was living a nightmare from which I couldn't wake up. That night in 1973, I knew that something was seriously wrong. My grandma and grandpa and a few uncles and aunts were surrounding us, quietly crying while hugging and blessing us. Grandma held each of us three children as tightly as she could. She didn't want to let us go. *Imana ibaje imbere kandi impe kuzosubira kubabona ntarashengera.* "May Imana lead your steps and grant me the privilege to see you before I die," she whispered through her sobs.

Where are we going? Why? How come our cousins are not coming with us? The questions where rolling in my young mind, although I dared not ask them aloud. That's not the Burundian way.

My oldest uncle helped my mom, my brother and my little sister climb into his truck that dark night. There were two or three other silhouettes by the truck who assisted with the little luggage we had. Everything was fuzzy and hushed. My uncle started driving to an unknown destination—unknown to me and my siblings but, for sure, known to him and my mom. Without any warning, the truck stopped.

My uncle came around the truck to be on the same side as we were. Shadows of two or three men I didn't know jumped from the back of the truck. My mom was still crying. The voices were kept very low during my uncle and my mom's long embrace. When it was our turn our beloved uncle hugged us one by one without saying a word. Then he stood there. He would quietly clear his throat often, an indication that he was trying to get rid of some kind of emotional knot.

Two men crossed the river very carefully to gauge its depth and take Mom's luggage to the other side. Then they came back with similar caution to the side where we were all standing. They held Mom's hand and helped her cross as we stood next to my uncle. The men returned to carry me and my sister on their shoulders as they crossed again. My feet and part of my legs were dangling in the river. I could feel the cold water, tree branches, twigs and who-knows-what creatures brushing my skin.

It didn't take very long before we reached a hut, and my mom knocked at the door and pleaded, "*Turasavye indaro. Turahunze,*" which means, "Please give us a place to stay through the night. We are fleeing."

Her words didn't mean much to me. I had no concept of "fleeing" and I was too young to understand. All I knew was how I felt. Whatever that word meant, it evoked a sense of imminent danger. Mom's shaking voice confirmed what I felt.

Someone opened the door of the little hut. I don't recall whether it was a man or woman. Just a kind soul showing humanity by opening a door to strangers in the middle of the night. I don't think there was much of an exchange between Mom and our guardian angel. She or he rolled out a small hand-woven mat, *ikirago*, for us in the entryway of the hut and let us crash on it. The mat was too small for all of us.

Mom helped us three children snuggle as close to each other as possible and covered us with her own traditional clothing, *ibitenge*. We kept our shoes and clothes on. She then sat against the rough dirt wall until the morning, with her hand stretched out to wrap all of us. Her arm never left us.

That journey was the first of four times that I would be forced to escape from intolerable or unsafe places, until finally I found a home in the USA. No matter how long I live, I will never forget the kindness of that unknown person who gave us a safe place to hide as we fled from the only home I had known to that date.

Laetitia, West Fargo, North Dakota[1]
(originally from Burundi)

Familiar Faces

In 1986, when I was 16, my mom sent me to live with my dad for the summer. I had made some poor choices and I guess she figured that getting me out of town and away from bad influences would help me get off the downward spiral I was on and get back on the right track. I cried the whole hour drive to my dad's house. I had to leave everything I knew, my brother and sisters, my mom, my home and all of my friends. I wasn't only angry, I was heartbroken. I felt like a failure. I knew I was a disappointment to my family and through my teenaged angst, I felt completely unloved.

A few weeks into my stay, my dad found me a job working a hot dog stand to help advertise a store's grand re-opening. Every morning we'd get up before dawn and we'd drive the 45-minute trip to drop me off before he headed to his own job. Day in and day out, I did nothing but sell hot dogs—10 cents apiece, eight hours a day. I had no interaction with my friends, and I had no interaction with my family, other than my dad. While I loved my dad dearly and he loved me, I felt lonely and sad and I just wanted to go home. One particular day, as I was dodging a hot dog that was being thrown at me by an unhappy customer, I hit an all-time low. How did things turn so bad, so fast?

But then, something unexpected happened—as I looked out into my line of customers, I saw two familiar faces. There, in the crowd, stood my Papa and my Uncle Dee. They had come to find me. My uncle, who was visiting from Colorado, and my Papa, who lived nowhere near there—jumped in the car and set out on a search. After scanning the beach for hours, they finally found my stand. There they were, suddenly ready to love on me. When I was feeling the loneliest and the most unloved—they found me. They didn't see a disappointment, they didn't see a failure. They saw me—their beloved niece and granddaughter. I had no idea they were coming but they showed up when I needed them most.

That is what love does—it shows up. It doesn't have to be a grand gesture, and it doesn't have to cost a dime, it just has to make its appearance.

Anita, Seal Beach, California

Welcome Home

I completed an application for my family to be resettled in the United States. We were refugees who had already been forced to live in three different countries, traveling from country to country, trying to find a new home. I prayed very hard that we would be accepted but I was skeptical about the probability of that happening. With less than 2 percent of refugees being considered for resettlement by all the countries participating in that humanitarian program, I did not believe that my family would be that lucky, especially given our status as "urban" refugees with some type of "stability" as compared to our counterparts living in much more desperation or destitution in camps all over the world.

I worried we wouldn't be considered a priority because we were not living in dire conditions. Because of this, I left a few questions blank on my application; one asked about a place we would prefer to be resettled if approved and the other inquired about possible family ties already in the U.S. With those two questions left unanswered, coupled with other factors, serendipity or karma brought us, one fine fall night, to the Red River Valley in the Midwest.

We came to Fargo looking for shelter, safety and opportunities. What we found was much more than that. Not only was the apartment our resettlement agency had secured for us new, spacious and in a nice part of town, but you could tell that everything we found inside waiting for us had been meticulously placed there in a loving and caring manner. There was food, milk and juice in the fridge, fruit on the counter, more dry and nonperishable food in the cabinets, the thermostat had been adjusted to a comfortably warm temperature, and there were towels on the rack in the bathroom and in the kitchen.

I had to hold my hands on my chest to keep my heart from stopping when I opened one of the three bedrooms to realize the single detail that still brings a tear to my face: The beds were made!

Exceeding our expectations from day one, Fargo gave us not only the refuge we so longed for but also the friends and family we had lost or left behind. Fargo gave us the kind of love we sometimes doubt can exist between strangers.

Laetitia, West Fargo, North Dakota[1]
(originally from Burundi)

Gentleman in Plaid

It was a crisp autumn afternoon in 2008, central Washington; the sun shone brightly against the changing leaves. As a newlywed, I wanted to have a hearty dinner ready for when my husband got off work, but I had some time to kill. The roast with veggies was brewing contently in the crock pot. Our two dogs, Buddy and Eva, both Labrador mixes, were in need of getting out so that's just what we did. The cool air felt refreshing in my lungs as I jogged for the first part of our outing. The area I normally walk in was busy with school children, so I took a different route. As I turned the corner next to a busy highway, both pups alerted me that something was amiss by flanking my sides and pressing their warm furry bodies against my yoga pants. Both of them growled low, hair raised on their backs. I started to look around.

That's when I saw him.

He was a large man, slicked back hair, black coat, white shirt, large hooked nose and black eyes that pierced me when we made eye contact. A chill ran down my spine. Trouble. We were close to home, but not close enough. I knew that if I started to run, the dogs would bolt, pulling me, and I could fall. I wrapped both leashes tighter around my hands, knuckles turning white with the hard grip. The cool refreshing air now burned my lungs. I couldn't get enough oxygen. My body felt like lead, each step harder to take. I could see our new home—the little fence that surrounds the property looked inviting. My goal was to make it home. Home meant safety. The pursuer was approximately 10 feet from me. Both dogs were pressing into my legs; I could barely move them. My heart pounded, adrenaline surged.

When I turned back to focus on my goal, an elderly man stood on the sidewalk, directly in front of me. He wasn't there just a second before. He had a kind face, balding head and a neatly pressed plaid shirt tucked into his pants.

"Excuse me, Ma'am, are you okay?" he asked, his voice clear and calm.

I turned to look at the man who was following me and watched as he did an about turn and started running the opposite way. Relief washed over me and I could no longer hold my emotions. Tears streaming down my cheeks, I turned to thank the elderly gentleman, but he was gone. I still do not know who he was, but I will never forget the act of kindness he offered to keep a stranger safe.

Stephannie, Kennewick, Washington

The Pool-Playing Messenger

I was playing pool alone in my living room when the clicking of the cue ball attracted a neighbor I'd never met and haven't seen since. He was an amazing pool player who could do magical things with a cue ball. We made small talk for a while, but eventually turned our conversation toward gold mining. In fact, we talked about gold mining for hours as we played. When he left later that night, I was completely infected with the world's worst (or perhaps best) case of gold fever. Even though I knew nothing about gold, motors or mining, I couldn't wait to turn my life upside down chasing an impossible dream. Everyone said I was crazy, but I didn't care.

Within a couple months, I'd sold or stored everything I owned, bought a dredge, wetsuit, tent and six months of dehydrated camp food. I packed it all in my car and moved to the LDMA (Lost Dutchman's Mining Association) camp on the Stanislaus River near Columbia in Northern California. It was a real mining camp, filled with dreamers and schemers just like me, smack in the middle of the Gold Rush country.

I'd never worked so hard in my life nor had so much fun doing it.

One day, while under water and scraping away the overburden supporting a truck-sized boulder, I saw a flash of color.

69

In a few minutes, a nugget fell free from the hard-packed sand. I broke the surface holding the biggest gold nugget I'd ever seen; I found a bit of gold, yes, but that was the least of the treasures. I found my confidence. I found God as He showered His blessings on me. I found my gratitude.

My pool-playing neighbor planted a seed. I never learned his name, but he changed my life forever.

Dave, Stanislaus River, California

PEOPLE ARE GOOD...

When They Make Others a Priority

Text Messages

I always thought to make a big impact in the world, you would need to take a year off work or personal responsibilities and set up clean water wells in a foreign country or start a non-profit organization to house the homeless or at least something of that magnitude. My friend Amy has taught me the extreme power demonstrated by one of her favorite quotes by Mother Teresa: "Not all of us can do great things. But we can do small things with great love."

Amy believes in the philosophy of small and deep when it comes to people interactions and making a difference. In her life as the mom, wife, neighbor and friend who can be called upon at any hour of the day, she understands that small things can make a life-changing difference for the people in her world. One particular instance came when I was traveling for work and was faced with a series of cross-country plane delays. I arrived on the East Coast at 3 a.m., got my rental car and drove alone to my hotel in a small town outside of Boston. I had to pick up a colleague at 7 a.m. and be at my best for a client meeting 30 minutes later. But how?

I was exhausted and had no idea how I was going to pull this off. That is when the texts started coming in. It was 5 a.m. where Amy lives so I know she had to set an alarm to help me through that groggy early morning. Clever messages, each one more helpful than the last, gave me my boost. "Take one step and then another," she'd say, along with a myriad of other humorous notes that had me laughing out loud. Not a big deal some might think but profound knowing you have a friend who is willing to come alongside this quintessential "non-morning" person and make a huge difference. Amy has changed my view of the kinds of gestures that make great impact in the world.

Maryanna, Boise, Idaho

Coach

The summers before my sophomore, junior and senior years of high school were spent in the gym developing my basketball skills. After being cut from a team in junior high, I knew two things: I had a lot to learn and being 6 feet 5 inches alone wasn't enough. Without me asking, Paul, the high school basketball coach, voluntarily drove 30 minutes from his house to the school—five days a week, three summers in a row—to meet me at the gym. We'd spend hours working on everything from footwork to shooting to ball handling. He developed my game and taught me a work ethic that I would carry with me both on and off the court. His dedication turned me into a player who would go on to play successfully at the collegiate level. This coach, my mentor, gave of himself, his time and his knowledge of the game, and, in doing so, set an example for the coach I would later become. Even though this coach is no longer with us, he is with ME. Every time I step on the court to coach a basketball game, he is with me. Every time I open the gym for a player to work on skill development, he is with me. It is in his honor and memory that I pay it forward.

Mark, Redding, California

Anxiety

A few years ago I found myself in a place I had never been. I was heading into middle school and suddenly filled with anxiety. My friend group had changed, I was working to keep my good grades, was overcommitted to two club sports—and no longer could eat or sleep. For months I wandered the house at night trying to find relief from my overactive mind. My parents would find me asleep in the hall, at the foot of their bed, or sprawled across the stairs. They were terrified by what was happening. I started to lose weight and my freckles suddenly were hidden by black circles under my eyes. They went into action and got me counseling and pulled me from soccer. I was grateful. But still, the anxiety stayed.

Around that time, a friend I had known a few years, but had not been close to, invited me to her home. Her mom, Michelle, asked me how I was doing, but I told her nothing of my troubles. My friend invited me again and again, and each time her mom checked in on me. Slowly, I was able to share my anxieties. She made me feel safe and never judged me or my worries. I felt the anxiety slipping away. Not only did I have a new dear friend, but also felt loved and cared for by her parents. They were a new support system that I didn't even know I needed. They became great friends with my parents and together they celebrated the successes I had as my appetite returned and my nights filled with sleep. I don't know how, but their interest helped me somehow. After about a year or so, I was back to my old self and my parents once again had their bed to themselves. This family will be a part of my life forever.

Elena, Boise, Idaho

The Driving Lesson

I was a teenager back in 1986 when my oldest sister married Greg. My new brother-in-law changed our family's dynamics considerably. He and I didn't always see eye to eye at first, but I saw him in a new light the day I had to follow him 10 miles into town in my sister's car for repairs. No one else was available to drive it in, and of course it was a stick shift which terrified me. I made it fine until I came to the four-way stop in town. I killed the engine repeatedly. Greg came to check on me and helped me get the car shifted into first. (I had it in third!) I was embarrassed and in tears by the time we arrived at the mechanic's and vowed to never drive a stick shift car again.

When we got home, instead of making fun of me or leaving me to wallow in self-pity, Greg asked me to get behind the wheel of his car, also a stick shift. Reluctantly, I did. That afternoon, he had me travel back and forth in my parents' driveway loop, starting and stopping until I was comfortable with the shift pattern. While stick shift cars will never be my vehicle of choice, I'll never forget my brother-in-law's kindness and patience in taking time out to teach me something new.

Cynthia, location unknown

The Boss

Disney has become very special to my son, Zeke, ever since he realized he shares the same birthday as Walt Disney. During our January 2017 trip to Disney World, Zeke, for fun, dressed up as Walt Disney. As we were waiting in line to ride Buzz Lightyear, one of the cast members, realizing that our son was honoring Walt, asked how many members were in our party. We told her the answer and she smiled and said, "Come with me." She led us around to the back of the ride and said, "It's not every day the boss comes to see us at work." As we were walking to a secret door, other cast members stopped and said, "Hello, Boss!" They even took our picture. Then the cast member escorted our whole party onto the ride where everyone gets off and we got to ride without any wait. The cast member surely has no idea how special she made my son feel that day. But I do. Little things can touch someone's life forever. This was one of those moments that our whole family will remember always.

Betsy, Naples, Florida

Digging Deep

My first in-person introduction to Maryanna was in Maui, Hawaii. If you happen to stumble across someone who will make a profound impact on your life, Maui is a nice place to do it! We had worked on a project together several years before, but only via email. So this Maui adventure afforded us time to chat and get to know one another. She was full of questions and seemed genuinely interested in me and my life.

Maryanna started to see something in me that I did not. She saw a capable woman with a story to tell. For years, I had been contemplating writing my own book and had spent significant time writing stories and even had spent time in a secluded cabin in Montana to write, hoping to discover where God was leading me. I thought He was calling me to write a book; however, I was at a crossroads and believed I didn't have a book worth writing.

In retrospect, I can see how Maryanna gently nudged my confidence; she had pulled information out of me without me feeling the tug. At the end of our time together, she asked me to consider something that could profoundly change my life. She said, "I'd love for you to meet my team. I want you to spend three days with us." She is the CEO of a publishing company and, somehow, she had gleaned enough information to know I had a book that needed to be written. She was determined to make it happen. For me, it felt like I was jumping off a cliff into thin air.

Because Maryanna was willing to listen to her instincts and take the time to get to learn about me, my life has been transformed. I have written my book and have shared my message with the world . . . all because a new friend was determined to dig deep.

Susan, Battle Lake, Minnesota[2]

The Car

Rick is a colossal guy. He's one of those father figures who always seems to show up at the right time with the right wisdom for my life. Since my dad passed away in 2009, Rick has been one of few people who have been vital in helping me make major life decisions. He seems almost placed in my life intentionally for that reason.

During the summer of 2014, I cleaned out my savings account to buy a home. It was a major investment but a smart one that I needed for my future. I knew I needed to start building the account again so I could do the next step: buy an engagement ring so I could propose to Lisa. I knew I would always love her and I wanted her ring to be a real sacrifice—something that she could take great pride in, so I had a grand figure in mind as to what I should spend. One morning, I heard a little voice in my head say *double it*. Having already forecasted till the end of the year to save the first amount, I thought that I had better come up with a new plan to get the money faster. And then the answer hit me.

Excited, I shared the new plan with my boss, Tim: "Tim, I have a plan—I can sell my car and get half of the money I need!"

A few weeks later Tim called to let me know a silent bene-factor had heard of my plan and wanted to give me a car to replace the one I was selling. It seemed surreal. Who would want to give me a car? I could think of a hundred people who needed and deserved it more. Moreover, I certainly didn't know of any rich uncles.

I soon became suspicious when I received an out-of-the-blue invitation to Rick's house. Upon arriving, I noticed a car I hadn't seen before. It had been detailed and its seats were newly upholstered. New tires and a full tank of gas. Rick had gone completely out of his way to give a gift good enough for an important dignitary. It was the cleanest car I had ever seen and he had spent time and money making it so. I cried when he gave it to me. He didn't know this, but he had chosen to give me the car on September 23, my dad's birthday. Now the gift was symbolic as well. I proudly drove that car until after our marriage and often thought of the profound impact that one act of kindness had on me.

Josh, Redding, California

Minnesota Vikings

The first time I met Anna was on a conference call. There were several other people on the call as well when I made a comment that I thought was quite funny. Instead of laughter, though, my quip was met with dead silence. Anna was the first person I was supposed to work with on my project, but after my failed attempt at humor, I was terrified to contact her.

For at least a couple of weeks, instead of calling Anna for answers to my questions that I was paying the company to answer, I called others and paid for their input. I admit, I was the irrational one at this point in time and finally corralled the courage to call Anna. To my utter astonishment, she was incredibly nice! She listened to what I had to say and even spent time off the clock to help me with the project. We became like two peas in a pod, working together, thinking together and developing an amazing project. Among many things, we talked about our favorite sports teams. When it came to the NFL, I was adamant about being a Minnesota Vikings fan and she was adamant about being a San Francisco 49ers fan. I guess no one agrees on everything.

The time came for the rubber to hit the road. We were going to meet in person. In the back of my mind, I still was harboring some hesitation due to the lack of an iota of sense of humor with the group on the initial phone call. One on one on the phone, Anna was fantastic and it was like we had known each other for years. Which Anna would I meet? The one who terrified me or the one who felt like a sister?

Anna offered to pick me up at the airport. She said I would know who she was which I took to mean that I should recognize her from her photo on the company website. As I left the airport security and looked at the mass of people waiting to find their friends and family, I did not need the picture from the website. Anna was the only person wearing a Minnesota Vikings shirt! That one act showed me how an inaccurate first impression can thwart the making of a true friendship.

SS, Minneapolis, Minnesota

The Call

I run a consulting business where I spend a good deal of time working with senior executives and their teams. Part of my job is helping leaders identify their company's core values, and one way I help draw these out is by having each leader share the names of their organization's high performers—one or two people who are so fantastic, such a good fit in the company that if they could find five more people just like them, they would hire them in an instant. After charting the names, I ask them to share the few characteristics that make them so great and so aligned to the organization. Those characteristics become descriptors that form a great starting point for identifying and agreeing on their company's core values.

Once that conversation and exercise are done, I often ask if those key employees—many of whom are named by multiple executives on the team—know how great they are and what great value they are to the company. Inevitably, the executives admit they could do better (usually *much* better!) at expressing gratitude and agree that it would be smart to make sure these key contributors are given recognition.

One of the first times I ever ran this exercise and asked that final question, the CEO of the large company I was working with admitted that they really needed to get better at giving recognition and then said, " . . . and it starts right here with me." He chose a woman from the list who had been named multiple times, got her phone number from a member of his leadership team, and called her on the speaker phone. Here is what he said when she picked up:

"This is Joe Smith (fictitious name), the CEO of our company, and I'm sitting here with my full executive team. We were talking about employees who are a great fit in the company, ones who are not only great performers but who are aligned with key behaviors that we need if we are going to be successful in the future. Your name came up *multiple* times by *multiple* members of my team. I thought you'd want to know, and I just want to say thank you for all the great things you do for our organization."

With a shaky voice, the woman responded that she was humbled, so very appreciative, and said she'd never received a call like this in 30-plus years of employment. There was not a dry eye in the room nor on the phone. I'm pretty sure she'll never forget that two-minute call—nor will any of those leaders! After seeing that impact, the executives agreed to make at least one call like that every time they had an offsite meeting. Every offsite meeting since that one, now many years later, they have followed through on that agreement, using that same simple act.

Mike, Tokyo, Japan

The Sewing Machine

My mom worked as a nurse in a clinic in Vallejo, California. One day a patient, Catherine, came into the clinic and my mom admired her dress. The woman explained that she had made the dress and that she used to be a seamstress when she lived in her home country of Jamaica. She had recently moved to the U.S. and hadn't been able to bring her sewing machine with her and wasn't able to afford to buy one.

Soon after their meeting, my mom continued to think about this lovely Jamaican woman. There had to be something she could do to help her. Scouring the thrift shops in our area, my mom finally found a used sewing machine at Goodwill. It was the perfect gift for her new acquaintance. It wasn't long before my mom began bringing her clothing in need of repair or requiring alterations. Catherine also could make clothing without a pattern, just by taking someone's measurements. Soon, she was making clothes for our family. Eventually Catherine was able to start a small seamstress business—all because someone, my mom, gave her an opportunity that came in the form of a used sewing machine.

Kate, Balboa Island, California

Home in a Car

I worked in the accounting department of a school district in the heart of Los Angeles. Usually, my days were spent paying bills or recording invoices, so rarely did I have much contact with the students. One day, a district manager, Bill, came into the office and was visibly shaken. Early that morning he saw a family of six—two parents and four boys—getting out of their car. He wouldn't have thought much of it except that he had seen those same six getting into the car very late the night before. It became clear the car was the family's home.

He wasn't sure what to do with the information but jumped into action. He started emailing and calling anyone he could think of . . . teachers, parents, administrators. By the end of the day, he had rallied enough support and resources to get the family into a long-term hotel. While that solved an immediate need, Bill knew it wouldn't help for long. He kept at it. By the end of the week, he had found the father a job within the school district. It wasn't a fancy job, but it was enough to keep the family off the streets and on their way to a more permanent home.

Rosalie, Cerritos, California

The Lawn Mower

Spring of 2013 was a particularly rainy one and I noticed the grass in my neighbor's yard had gotten a little out of hand. I remember hearing the sound of a riding mower sputtering loudly and the voices of two women shrieking in panic. I walked to my fence to see what all the commotion was and saw my elderly neighbor and her grown daughter trying to get that poor mower unstuck from a muddy spot in their yard. They kept flooding the engine, which eventually died. I felt bad but I knew I would be of no use to them, and truth be told, didn't relish the thought of getting all muddy myself. I left the poor ladies fighting with the mud and obstinate contraption and went in to start dinner. Unbeknownst to me, my son-in-law, Scott, heard the whole thing while working in our shop. After finishing dinner preparations, to my surprise I heard the lawn mower running perfectly, so I went out to see how things were going.

As I walked by the shop I noticed my son-in-law's muddy clothes. He had hopped the fence and came to the rescue of my dear neighbors. He was just being his kind self, not even knowing that my neighbor's husband was suffering with Parkinson's and could no longer keep his lawn mown himself. It has been four years since that act of kindness. Since then my precious neighbor lost her husband, sold the house and moved. Before she left we shared a special time of visiting and she told me of how it meant the world to her when she saw Scott coming to the rescue of two distressed damsels.

Angela, Molalla, Oregon

Gideons Bibles

In 2014, a 75-year-old man, Bob, moved into our apartments where I am the landlord. After his first wife died, he quickly remarried. Two months later, he was divorced. She took everything. His life, up to that point, apparently had been one disaster after another. Not even his children spoke with him. His health declined quickly and he knew he wouldn't be around forever. Bob thought long and hard about the purpose of whatever life he had left. Despite his faith in Christ, life had always been about Bob. One morning he woke up and told himself from now on life would be about helping others. But where to start? Can you just . . . change?

Bob found the address for the local chapter of Gideons International and wandered into the office. After filling out paperwork, he headed home. Soon, they called him with an emergency—Bibles needed to be delivered. Could he, newly approved to help, do it? He loaded his car with a box of Bibles and started his new life. The Bible was always in his grasp as he made his deliveries.

His hands shook with nerves when he asked me (practiced on me) if he could put a Gideons Bible in our clubhouse. He started thinking of new places he could put Bibles. Who knows when someone would pick it up and read? His health began to strengthen. If it was so easy to find places for Bibles, why not try something else? He wandered into a nearby assisted living with a checkerboard under one arm, a box of pieces in his other hand, and looked at all the bored people.

"Can I ask if anyone wants to play?" He said to a nurse.

The friendless, hopeless Bob now had friends everywhere. Near his son was an orphanage that needed a janitor and had a bed for pay. He took the job and moved, and began reconciling with his once estranged son. The Bible he gave us still sits in our clubhouse, reminding me it's never too late to make a difference in people's lives.

Peter, Boise, Idaho

One Day at a Time

During my last year of community college, I worked as a full-time nanny for a family with four kids. I was the first person in my family to go to college and felt pressure all around especially as my long days became consumed by my job as well as writing assignments for my classes. These, along with the constant reminder of a childhood trauma, left me emotionally frail. Delia, my boss at the time, had her own struggles. Just before I began working for her family, her career in law enforcement was cut short when she'd broken her hip at work. I marveled at her attitude. She had endured surgery to replace her hip and was left with metal in her leg—rods that would remain in her bones forever. She was not even 40 years old. But nothing stopped her. She remained positive, day in and day out. One day when she saw me struggling with school and writing and general life pressures, she explained how she coped. She told me that the only thing I could do was to take "one day at a time."

Her attitude made little sense to me. I wanted to deal with everything all at once, but that just made my stress even worse. Her one-day-at-a-time motto seemed nice in theory but impossible in reality. As the days and weeks of the year melted by, Delia listened to me as I shared about life and how

I was working through it. After a year with Delia's family, I transferred to a university and my job ended. We stayed in touch, but I lived a few hours away on campus so we didn't see each other very often.

One day, after a tense situation with one of the girls who lived in my dorm, I found myself overcome with major anxiety. I took a deep breath, looked at myself in the mirror, and said, "It's okay, Krista. Just get through today." I shocked myself, because it was the first time I truly believed that I could survive *one day at a time*. That is a gift I have carried with me over all the years since then. I'm so thankful for Delia's words.

Krista, California

The Art Projects

It was July 2007. I was scheduled to teach kindergarten in the fall. Excited for the new school year ahead, I visited my classroom to prepare. I thought about the little lives that would grace the room with cuteness, creativity and curiosity. For three years I'd worked for this prosperous community. The high expectations brought pressures to produce elaborate art projects, which motivated me to open my personal pocketbook. I was happy to do it and in most circumstances, I never thought twice about it. My husband and I had good steady jobs, which meant that I was free to find special projects on my own. Then everything changed.

Suddenly, I was the only one employed. I nervously dealt with the fact that I had no choice but to use only those supplies offered by the school. Every day, in my prayer time, I thanked God that we were still financially afloat. I mentioned to God that I really wanted to provide fine art projects for my students. Days passed. I continued to pray. The summer months flew by. My husband remained unemployed, but thankfully, we could still eat and were able to stay on top of our bills. Soon, the first day of school arrived. After a week or so I started feeling the burden of the art projects. Those pricey projects were ahead of me, but my story was the same.

The very next morning, a parent met me at the door of my classroom. She handed me a small white envelope and said, "Thank you for a great first week of school!" I thanked her for the kind words, then quickly placed the envelope on my desk and began the day. Then, like most days, in a flash, our day was over. I said my farewells and made my way back to my desk. Waiting for me was the envelope.

As I read, the words were a jumble. I was in shock. I rubbed my eyes for a minute, brought the note into a stronger light and stared at the words again: "Dear Mrs. Gentry, thank you for a great first week! Please use this craft store gift card for $500 to buy art supplies or whatever you need for the class."

I couldn't believe it! That was quite enough to buy supplies for the entire school year! This parent had no idea of my current situation, yet kindness graced me and she was the catalyst! In that moment, I thanked God for His goodness and the extravagant kindness shown to me that day.

Jennifer, California

The Paycheck

When my grown daughter received her very first "real" paycheck, she was so excited she invited me out to lunch at the local Asian restaurant. Our server was a friendly young woman and we chatted about her family and life in a small American town. She had mentioned in the conversation about missing her family in her own country and how it had been years since she had seen her mother. After finishing our meals we walked outside to leave but my daughter excused herself and headed back into the restaurant. When she came back out I asked her what she was doing. She simply replied that she just wanted to bless that sweet girl. I asked what she did and she said she gave her the remainder of her paycheck so she could go home and see her mom.

I have to admit, at first, I was a little shocked and concerned. She could sense my thoughts immediately and simply said, "Mom, I see my family every day and I can always make more money. I can't imagine being in a foreign country without family to support me and a mother to love me."

Stunned by her reply I shut my mouth and walked toward the car. Before we even got to the car the sweet little waitress ran out weeping and thanked my daughter for her generosity, saying she had never had anyone do anything like this before. We were both teary-eyed as we pulled away. I was so proud of my young, tenderhearted daughter. She saw a need and filled it.

Angela, Molalla, Oregon

Cart Full of Groceries

I was having a conversation with my daughter and her best friend about being happy. After a bit, I found myself telling (well, actually pleading) with them to hear me out.

I said, "Do you girls really want to know the quickest way to being happy?"

"Yes!" they laughed.

"The quickest way to happiness is always to find a way to serve others. Always. Serve. Meet a need. Be loving. Show people they matter. Without any expectations. Serve and you will see happiness grow right where you are standing."

Fast forward to today. It was a monster of a Monday. I spilled hot oatmeal on myself, first thing in the morning. I forgot to pack a few forms my kids needed for school. I ended up being late for my favorite class at the gym. I butt-dialed two people while I was vacuuming. I drove all the way to Albertsons with my daughter in 5 o'clock traffic only to realize when I parked that I had forgotten my wallet. Frustrated, we went home, got the wallet and chose to go to Fred Meyer instead. I went on to fill my cart with stuff we desperately needed for the week and for tonight's dinner and beyond. We found a checkout line that was moving fast and things were finally coming together. I was thinking *go pick up my son, get the groceries put away, make dinner, bathe the kids. Maybe the day is not a complete loss.* With my food rung up and bagged, I went to run my card and it was declined. The checker asked me to run it again and it was declined a second time. I panicked inside. *How could this be? We just put money in the account.* But that was the way the whole day had been. I had a cart full of groceries and no other way to pay. I immediately grabbed my phone to call my husband but was greeted by his voicemail. Great.

A gal in her thirties standing right behind me in line stepped up toward me and said, "Let me go ahead and pay for your groceries. Seriously, don't stress. I have been there and my husband would be in complete agreement with me on this. Let me do this for you." I stared at her.

I quickly said, "Thank you so much. You are too kind, but I can't let you do that! Have you seen the amount?"

She replied, "I insist. Consider this an act of kindness and promise me you'll return the favor by paying it forward to someone else."

Then she came over to me and gave me a hug. I thanked her profusely. Feeling a mix of humility and embarrassment, I walked out the door with my daughter. I was not speaking. I couldn't really catch up with what had just transpired. Before we even got to the car, she quietly asked, "Mom, is that what you meant by serving others? Is that woman a happy woman?"

Talk about a real-life, full-circle moment. As my dad would say, "You can't make this up." God, in the form of a woman with curly brown, beautiful hair, a complete stranger, came right up to me that night and reassured me that He cared about the details of my life.

Beth, Meridian, Idaho

The Surprise Box

One day, around 2011, a small, cubed box arrived on my doorstep. Someone had drawn stick figures of me on each side of the box. One side had me driving my minivan, one stick figure was lifting dumbbells, another side showed me singing. I opened the box and found that it was from a friend who wished to be anonymous. She had filled it with a new Starbucks mug, a few chocolates and a Burt's Bees lip balm. My heart was so happy. Who was this friend who seemed to "see me?" Who was this friend who cared enough to draw pictures of me all over a gift box filled with goodies? Finally, after a few weeks, the giver admitted that she had left it for me. Our friendship grew to share many years of memories, laughter, heartache and encouragement. She will never truly know how that gift resonated in my heart. I soared from the knowledge that my life was making a difference worth drawing about.

Cara, Redding, California

The Belly

It was hot. And crowded. The bus system for Washington State University in Pullman, Washington, in 2003 ran on time, picking up students who lived off campus. The start of the school year was underway and the late afternoon heat in the Palouse was stifling. By the time I had gotten onto the bus, it was standing room only. My heavy bag dug into my shoulder. My other hand awkwardly clutched the warm metal handhold. The sweaty smell of young adults was nauseating. I was hungry, needed more coffee, and had a lot of studying to do for my new classes. My mind was full of the outlines, homework and other projects I needed to accomplish. I was not in the best of moods and the crowds were not helping. The bus made one last stop at the edge of campus. The students shuffled back to allow a newcomer on, bodies pressing into me.

I could see the lady who slowly stepped on. She looked frazzled, juggling multiple bags strapped to her body and a large belly protruded in front of her. It was the Teacher's Assistant from my Econ class. I immediately felt bad for her. All of my troubles seemed insignificant compared to the pregnant lady in a standing-room-only bus. She tried to protect her belly with one hand while desperately reaching for the high handhold. Students unavoidably bumped into her as the bus pulled into traffic.

"Stop! Please stop the bus!" a large booming voice said from behind me. The bus driver pulled over. All of us standing almost toppled into each other as the driver asked over the intercom what was wrong. "Here, lady in the front, please take my seat." I turned to see one of the largest men I have ever laid eyes on stand up. His huge frame had to duck to avoid hitting the top of the bus. Everyone standing made a path for her. When she sat down, she started to cry. The only thing she said, in a small voice, was "thank you." As the bus moved, the man who stood hit his head a few times but never complained. I was in awe of how this simple gesture of giving up a seat could really impact someone. Chivalry is not lost.

Stephannie, Kennewick, Washington

Bottles of Water

At 92 years old, my dad was still loving life. He had suffered a stroke and a few bouts of pneumonia, but nothing could stop him from enjoying the ball game (Go Angels!) or a good plate of spaghetti or a stroll around the block. One particularly hot Los Angeles day, he still wanted to get outside for his routine walk. While we knew there was some risk in this because he hadn't fully recovered from the stroke or the pneumonia, we thought, he is 92 and wants to walk! His caregiver and I attached him to his walker and off we went. He liked to walk the full block, which is about a quarter mile, but we thought this would be pushing it. Dad insisted! After all, he had walked this path hundreds—maybe even thousands—of times.

But at the end of our street, only a few steps in, Dad was already breathless, panting even. We sat him down on the corner wondering how we would get him home. It wasn't far, but we certainly couldn't carry him. That's when a stranger from across the street ran out to us with three bottles of cold water. She didn't know us but could see we were in a situation. Several minutes and his full bottle of cold water later, Dad was good to go, ready to continue on his walk. Water on a hot day may not seem like a lot to everyone, but to my Dad, it was a tiny act that helped him hang on—one more day—to those things he loves.

Vince, Danville, California

Holy in the Ordinary

Last November, I discovered an extraordinary, ordinary person in an airport bathroom. While waiting for my flight, I visited the ladies room. As one does. There was a line (as usual) and as I waited, I was slightly outside of the restroom. I couldn't actually see the stalls yet but I could hear a lot of activity inside. I rounded the corner and saw a woman in a staff uniform, greeting each person as they made their way to a stall to do their business. The Charlotte airport employed a bathroom attendant. But she wasn't just greeting women, wiping down the counter or handing out paper towels and mints. After every single person exited a stall, she would quickly jump in the stall, spritz the toilet with cleaner and wipe it down. This woman's day was spent literally wiping down toilets, in front of a crowd. Let me rephrase that so I can make myself absolutely clear: She was constantly cleaning toilets. In a public restroom. Public. Toilets. For hours. And that's not the most amazing part. She was doing it joyfully, with speed, efficiency and with a spring in her step. She cleaned like she was receiving a free trip to Disneyland for every toilet she wiped down. Each person waited a few seconds longer than normal to do their business to allow her to do hers.

When it was my turn, I passed her as I slipped into my freshly cleaned stall, looked into her eyes and whispered, *thank you.* She answered back with a chipper, *you're welcome,* then welcomed the next person who entered the restroom and jumped into the next open stall to quickly freshen it up for the next woman waiting in line. Every so often she would take a quick break from toilet cleaning to wipe the counter dry. Because the casual user can't be bothered with wiping away the water they splash everywhere, she did that for us. In a place built around schedules and stress, where strangers come and go and pass each other without a second thought, here was holy in the ordinary.

Stephanie, Norman, Oklahoma

The Fishing Trip

I have always loved fishing. Given the opportunity, I'd fish in any type of water, for any type of fish, in any season of the year. Every other summer, my Uncle Chris and Grandpa Dave would fly to some remote location in Canada and spend an entire week fishing for pike or anything else they could set their hooks in. I have always wanted to go on one of their trips with them but I was young and they were very expensive. In early 2017, my uncle called my mom to ask if I could join them on the next trip they were planning. He said that he and my grandpa would pay for everything, and the only thing needed was a "Yes!" and a passport. My parents gave both.

In the summer of 2017, I boarded the first of many planes that would lead me to my uncle, my grandpa and my cousin, Jack. Our adventures in Canada were waiting. I could not be more grateful for the time with my family, the trip and the people who planned and paid to turn the dreams of a boy with a fishing pole into a reality.

Tanner, Redding, California

Forty Dollars

Those parents who have a teenage daughter in their home know the fun of watching their child experiment with makeup. They research the best facial wash, eye concealer and mascara. After a ton of such research, my 14-year-old daughter, Ellie, asked if we could take a drive to the mall to shop at Sephora. She had $40 in cash that she had received for her birthday. I dragged her younger brother and sister along.

We arrived in Sephora, but Ellie wanted to take her time, so the rest of us cruised the mall. About 30 minutes later we connected back up. Ellie wore a smile that I didn't quite understand. She then told us of her moment of panic when she went up to the register to pay. She discovered the $40 was no longer in her pocket. Her heart starting racing. She then explained to the girl behind the counter what must have happened.

To Ellie's surprise, the girl said, "Well, this $40 must be yours. Someone found it on the floor and brought it to us."

I was dumbfounded that she had her money back! I tried to explain to her how lucky she was, but I'm not sure she realizes that there was someone "good" in that store that day.

Lisa, Boise, Idaho

Turning 80

My mom and her friends all turned 80 last year. As they did every year, 80 schoolmates chose a date and place to meet to celebrate. But this time was different. One of the friends had a special request: pay this forward. "Pay what forward?" they asked. The friend gave each of the 79 others a $100 bill. She asked them to do something good with the money, and then write to her about what they did. She told them they could donate the money to a favorite charity, give it to someone in need, or anything that struck them. There was no right or wrong thing to do. She thought it would be fun to see what that $8,000 could do to change the world.

Krissy, Los Altos, California

Elvis

Despite getting sometimes ridiculed for it, my status as a long-time Elvis Presley fan is well known among my friends, family and students. Posters of Elvis decorate the walls of my high school classroom and I even work tidbits about his life and career into my lesson plans! Through the thoughtfulness of my friend, Becky, one of my most memorable gifts came as a result of my Elvis fan status.

Becky served as a parent chaperone on a middle school field trip to Memphis in 2003, where I took my students to see an exhibit of the Titanic and then a tour of Graceland. On the bus trip home, Becky and I were seatmates and, among other things we talked about, she asked me about my Elvis obsession. In particular, she wondered about some of the memorabilia I had collected over the years. After describing a few special things I'd collected, I despondently recollected how a special souvenir newspaper that I'd kept since the week Elvis died had been mistakenly thrown out by my mother while cleaning out the closet of my childhood bedroom.

Several years passed and my friendship with Becky grew. One day in 2006, while going about a normal school day, I got a call from the receptionist asking me to come to the school's front office because I had a visitor. I was perplexed about who it could be, but as I didn't have students at the time, I left my classroom and hurried to the office. As I got closer, I saw Becky, standing in the hallway with a bag in hand, her smile as bright as Elvis' gold suit. She reached out to give me a hug, then thrust the bag in my hand.

"Here," she blurted, "I know it's late for your birthday, but I got it as soon as I could."

Puzzled and intrigued, I opened the gift bag, reached in, and pulled out a yellowed newspaper wrapped in plastic. THE newspaper. The very same edition of the very same souvenir newspaper from the week Elvis died. The one that I'd been embarrassed to admit I was mad at my mother for throwing away. She had searched high and low on the Internet and found a copy and bought it for me! Some may think this is silly, but this gift is a treasure to me.

Becky taught me that day that she valued this small thing because it mattered to me. She helped me realize that friends do not always have all interests in common but that they should find ways to know each other and take time to show those they love—sometimes in tangible, even seemingly superficial ways—that they are thinking about them and the things that bring them joy.

Robin, Madison, Alabama

Spider Monkey

To me, a true friend is like a spider monkey—stuck to you in happy times and sad. On August 18, 2016, the much anticipated—and equally dreaded—day came when I had to drop my daughter off for her freshman year of college. Being the firstborn and my only daughter, she and I have always been close. As the time drew near, I tried to be strong for her but the reality of coming home without her started to sink in. I remember reading an account of a famous actor dropping his son off at college and then pulling over to the side of the road so he could bawl his eyes out. I was hoping to avoid that kind of drama myself. Talk about wishful thinking! The very thought of her not being just down the hall from me in her childhood home brought me instantly to tears. Luckily, my dearest friend, Melissa, anticipated that very thing . . . and more.

She hired a babysitter for her four kids, insisted on driving us the many hours to the college, organized the unpacking, and helped me make sure my girl was settled and comfortable. She was solid that day, the rock that I wasn't. She was there with kind words and anything else I needed. Her strength kept me from making a scene, from begging my daughter to change her mind! To stay home with me! (Who needs college?!!) Melissa helped me let my daughter grow up. She never left my side. She was my spider monkey.

N.S., Chico, California

PEOPLE ARE GOOD...

Even When Parenting Isn't

Liquid Gold

My mother loves to tell me the story of the day she brought me home. I was adopted before I was born but was unable to leave my country for two months. By the time I made it to the United States, I still weighed in around six pounds. My legs were like "toothpicks" she said, and she and my dad were frightened to bathe or dress me for fear of "snapping a limb in half."

She shared these fears with everyone as she and my dad fed me continually, hoping to add some girth. As my good fortune would have it, one of my mom's closest friends, Michele, birthed her own baby only two days before I was born. Anthony was a hungry fellow so she always had plenty of breast milk. She and my mom were determined to fatten me up, so Michele would bring over little bags of liquid gold. Her boy couldn't begin to eat all that she had, so she generously shared with me. Before we knew it, I was 10 pounds and then 15! These kinds of gifts can't be given by just anyone. I know my life started off well because Michele loved me like my mom did.

Gabriella, Boise, Idaho

Beautiful Mess

It was another sleepless night holding my toddler while she nursed. All night. Again. My shoulder ached. My head hurt. And all the little ones were up and ready for the day. I needed coffee fast. And some ibuprofen. Stumbling into the kitchen I fired up the Keurig and downed the slow-acting pills. I was out of eggs and I didn't have enough milk to feed them all cereal. So we settled on granola bars, grapes and string cheese. I gulped my coffee so fast it scalded my throat on the way down. At least the kids didn't seem to mind having a scavenger-type breakfast. The day progressed rapidly.

As soon as the kitchen was clean, it was time to fix lunch. My oldest daughter was having a fit because her favorite shorts were dirty and apparently none of the other 20 pairs she owned would work. The middle two were fighting over who knows what. The youngest wanted to nurse again. In the midst of reigning down justice and order in the chaos, I forgot about lunch and the noodles became a lump of scalded mush in the bottom of my brand-new pot. I came unglued. Tears of frustration streamed down my face as I tossed the pot, mush and all, into the sink and dropped to the floor. One day. I just needed one day to go according to plan. The laundry was never ending. The kitchen was a place of constant need; cook, clean, cook, clean. Over and over again. There was always pee on the toilet seat. The ceiling fans and baseboards always needed dusting. And there were toys everywhere. All the time.

On my feet, I worked from the moment I rolled out of bed until late at night when I finally collapsed back into it. Yet I never felt a sense of completion. I sat on my floor crying, frustrated at my shortcomings, and couldn't believe the state I'd found myself in. All I'd ever wanted to do was be a wife and a mom. I was doing exactly what I'd dreamed of. And I sucked at it. I simply couldn't do it right. I wanted to be the mom that had the clean house with the empty laundry room. The mom who baked everything from scratch and never screamed at her kids. But I fell short. Way short. Then my doorbell rang.

I was so ashamed when I opened the door to find Jane, my Sunday school teacher, and the tears poured out again. She hugged my neck and waited patiently while I got the children occupied so we could chat. She'd brought a Bible study that God had laid on her heart to share with me called Beautiful Mess, and she said that I'm exactly the mother God had chosen for my kids. This truth brought amazing perspective. I may not be a perfect mother, but God chose me to be theirs.

Brandi, Oxford, Alabama

The Weekend Away

In March of 2001, my son, Casper, was 4 months old, my daughter, Julia, was 17 months old, and I was suffering from postpartum depression. Upon returning from work one evening, my husband found me in disarray. I was exhausted. My normally tidy home wasn't. And, the time I loved sharing with him once he walked through the door was proving to be less and less. With an expression of helplessness he looked at me not knowing what to do and finally asked, "Do you need to get away?"

With my Bible and our best friend's lake house as my destination, Jesus and I spent a beautiful weekend together. When I returned, my precious husband with both babies in his arms was my local hero. After 25 years of marriage, I often still thank him for saving me that day.

Christine, Clarkston, Michigan

The Rescue

Our dream to adopt a child from Mexico came true in 2007 when we brought our newborn baby girl home. We were instantly in love with her and knew she was made for our family. My 7-year-old daughter welcomed her with loving, open arms, and my 5-year-old son greeted her each day with a "good morning, Sweetheart." We all were smitten.

But then the crying kicked in. For nearly two years, our precious newborn would not stop screaming. If she was awake, she was wailing. We tried everything we could think of to soothe her. We snuggled her, fed her, changed her, took her to numerous doctors, sought the advice of anyone who would listen. Our family of five was on edge.

A dear friend of mine had a daughter who was just two weeks older than our baby and continually offered to bring our baby to her home to play with her daughter and, really, to give us a break. The crying did not phase her. (And, if it did, she never let it show!) Our baby visited their home dozens of times. That time away gave the rest of the family a chance to reconnect, gather our thoughts, and, sometimes even take a nap!

Finally, after six different doctor exams, we learned our baby had ear pain that was unbearable. A quick trip to an ear/nose/throat specialist changed her overnight! Nine years later, these two babies are still best friends. They see each other often and enjoy the many memories they have made over the years. Each time I see these girls together, I think of the mom who rescued me time and time again.

Anna, Boise, Idaho

Dad's Call

When I left Oklahoma for Colorado, it was the first time I had really been away from home. While I always knew that my dad loved me, I am not sure I knew the true extent of what that meant. I was working at DaySpring at the time we packed up the truck—his camper had all of my worldly possessions—including a rocking chair that was roped to the back. We looked like the Clampetts from *Beverly Hillbillies*. My Aunt Wanda and I drove out to Colorado Springs to try to find an apartment. My dad was going to come later and bring the furniture. My mother was away on business in New Orleans. Aunt Wanda and I found an apartment and called Dad and told him it was time to come out. He made his way to a hotel where we all met. That night, when I heard him speaking to my mother on the phone, I saw something I had never seen. My father had tears spilling out. He tried to control himself, but eventually the sobs made their way out, too. I had no idea what was happening.

The next morning, he packed up his things and said his goodbyes. I was heartbroken to see my dad go. I was crying and needed comfort, so I called my mom from a payphone at the 7-Eleven. She calmed me by saying she'd visit in a couple of months, but also by sharing something I hadn't ever known: "You know you are his favorite, right?"

I don't think I knew until that moment the depths of his love for me. Not only did he love me, I brought him joy whether I was good or bad. He's 94 now and his eyes light up when I walk into a room. I am the apple of his eye. That kind of love changes you. It allows you to accept the deep love of God. It gives you strength and wings and joy and hope. When I tuck him in now, he says I'm his inspiration. But really, he must know, that he is MY inspiration. He is everything that is good in my world and I am so very glad that God chose him for me.

Jeane, Welch, Oklahoma

PEOPLE ARE GOOD...

When Reflecting the Face of Jesus

A Rotisserie Chicken

It was over five years ago, but I remember it well. It all started with a chicken. I'd had one of those days, the kind where everyone needed something and nothing went right. I was tired and discouraged, just needing to know God still saw me and He still cared. A knock came on the door, and I cringed. "Jesus, I can't take much more," I muttered as I peeked outside. I opened the door and found a friend from church was on my front porch, holding a deli rotisserie chicken. She'd picked up dinner for her family, and heard God tell her to buy an extra chicken for my family. She had picked up a pre-packaged salad and a loaf of bread, figuring if God wanted me to have a chicken, I might as well have a couple of sides, too! I could sense her uncertainty. I mean, who just shows up unexpectedly with a roasted bird? I thanked her for her thoughtfulness, letting her know that the last thing I wanted to do was worry about dinner. We hugged, and she left. With the door closed, I broke down and sobbed. God saw me, and He loved me. How did I know? He sent me a chicken.

Deena, location unknown

The Smile

It was my first day back to work after a 12-week maternity leave. I was headed to drop off our baby girl for her first day of daycare. I was a wreck. My emotions were all over the place and I was questioning both our decision for me to return to work as well as the daycare we had chosen, back when I found out I was pregnant.

It was early morning on a Monday in January 2000. I remember it vividly. I was at a two-lane stoplight waiting for the light to turn red when a truck pulled up beside me on the passenger side of my car. The tears were running down my face and I remember praying that this would all be okay. As the truck stopped I glanced through the passenger side of the window and a kind man locked eyes with me and gave me a smile that still resonates in my memory. I don't know who this man was but I do believe that God sends all kinds of people to our lives who have the ability to share something as simple as a smile. Of course, I was still emotional and heartbroken to leave my baby, but I knew God would be with her just as He was with me.

Deb, Boise, Idaho

The Prayer

On Wednesday, May 5, 2016, I was at the hospital while another surgical procedure began on my sweet daddy. I was unsettled this time more than usual. We were sitting in the waiting room with family in shock and disbelief this was happening again. I couldn't sit anymore with them staring at me as I wept. I got up to take a walk and my husband suggested coffee. He understands my need for a purpose when I am really hurting. I approached the coffee counter slowly, finding the menu. When I stepped up this beautiful woman asked me what I would like today. I remember ordering my coffee between sobs and sniffles. She fixed my coffee, took my money and came out from behind the counter. The most wonderful thing happened. She handed me a box of Kleenex and asked why I was crying. When I finally was able to share with her, she said to me "I can tell you are a believer in the One true God. There isn't anything your daddy can't handle with Jesus. May I pray for him, and for you?"

I stood in the small area under the stairs while she laid her hand on my shoulder. She prayed the best, most confident prayer I have ever heard in my life. She didn't fill her prayer with a generic request to heal my dad. She filled it with love, gratitude—and healing for my heart. She spoke of truth and suffering out of love and sacrifice. She spoke of God's will. She spoke to Jesus as if He were standing right there with us. And I realized, He was. This woman gave me a huge tight hug, and went back to work. I never even got her name. She was the Jesus I needed in those moments. I was uncertain. Our future was up in the air. I knew the test results would be difficult to accept. I knew in my heart it was going to be bad this time. But the kindness of a stranger, to step out from behind her coffee counter and pray fervently over me, was enough to give me hope.

I think of her from time to time, and it makes me wonder if I could ever be so bold to do the same. To serve others unselfishly, so unashamed. To be Jesus to someone in the light of day, right when they need Him most.

Angie, Jamestown, Ohio

The Bicyclists

It was an early Sunday morning in June 2017, the temperature was rising way too fast, and our Missouri humidity wasn't helping matters. My husband and I were headed to church when we passed a couple stranded alongside the road. Their bicycles—which appeared to be their only mode of transportation—lay in a heap in the grass. We drove by so quickly I couldn't tell if they'd had an accident or were simply taking a quick rest from biking our Ozark hills. I waved sympathetically at them, but my thoughts drifted onward to the day's plans, which included Bible study and visiting with family. To my shame, I forgot about the stranded cyclists a moment later as we pulled into the church parking lot. My husband did not.

"I'm going to go back and see if they need some help," he said simply.

"But what about church? We'll be late," I replied.

"You go on without me. I won't be long. I want to check on them." My husband has a heart for cyclists, even though it's been years since he's been on a bike. He used to be an avid mountain biker before our first baby came along and his hours at work increased. Nowadays, he supports his biking friends and talks shop with them. He volunteers at trail building days and dreams of the next chance he'll get to take his old bike out for a spin. Needless to say, I was not surprised when the words came out of my husband's mouth. Of course he was going to go back to check on the cyclists. It was just like him to put his own plans aside and help someone else with theirs. I nodded in agreement and we parted ways. I headed in to church and he headed back to the strangers.

As it turned out, the man and wife along the roadside were from Germany. They had come to America to bike across the entire country. They had started in Washington D.C. and were headed all the way to Oregon when their tire was damaged beyond repair in middle-of-nowhere Missouri. My husband volunteered to drive them to the nearest city, which was over an hour away to get a new bike tire. On the way, he enjoyed visiting with the German man about their shared interests in biking and computers. Only God could bring kindred spirits like that together from different continents. If it hadn't been for my husband's help, the couple would have been stranded for days in our small town until they could order a new tire. Church was over by the time my husband arrived, but it didn't matter. "He had the opportunity to be Jesus' hands and feet today," my mom reminded me. And she was right. My husband saw a need and stepped up, not only helping two people a long way from home, but also inspiring me to keep my eyes and heart open every day to the needs of others.

Savanna, Hartville, Missouri

The Tithe

In a difficult season in our lives, our best friends taught us a beautiful lesson on tithing. This Biblical discipline was something my husband and I often resisted. In early 2002, with two small babies, we were suffering from a job loss and a wrongful law suit that left us struggling financially. Our friends had recently sold their house and as faithful followers of Jesus Christ they had set aside their tithe from the profit of their home to give to their church. However, they received direction from God to hold on to the money and that He would show them where He would have them give. So within a few months, we found ourselves in our situation and they found their response from God. With love and compassion they were obedient to the Lord's call and offered us a remarkable gift, one that changed the trajectory of our walk of faith. We now tithe faithfully and the Lord has given us many opportunities to follow the example of our dear friends.

Christine, Clarkston, Michigan

The Boise State Fan

I was going through a tough time in college during my junior year. I had my heart broken by my high school sweetheart and was in many toxic relationships with girls I thought were my friends. I knew deep down I needed a change but didn't know how to make a move. I prayed all summer about whether to move home or stay where I was. I had never wanted to give up and that's exactly what I felt like I was doing by finally deciding to move home to Boise, Idaho. I was so disappointed in myself and although I knew it wasn't all my fault for feeling so down, I continued to take the blame. I had to sell everything, which surprisingly happened easily. First went my bed, then lots of furniture. Eventually, all I had left to sell was my truck, but I wasn't getting any calls on it. I reposted to Craig's List one last time before trying to figure out a plan B. That day the phone finally rang. The couple on the phone asked why I had an Idaho number but lived so far away from home. I felt it an odd question and couldn't shake the strange feeling it gave me, but still headed toward the designated meeting place.

I parked and got out of the truck. As the family emerged from their car, the first thing I noticed was their young son, who was wearing a bright orange Boise State football jersey. I couldn't believe it. I was completely on the opposite side of the country and had never seen one person wear anything Boise State related. Of course, it was the first thing I said to them. "Wow, a Boise State fan here?" They laughed. Their completely out-of-the-blue connection to Boise validated everything for me about my life. They were kind people who sensed my need for a Boise connection during a hard time in my life. Their son hugged me, excited to interact with someone from Boise who shared his passion for Boise State football. After we signed papers and completed the transaction, the mom hugged me really tight. She told me everything was going to be okay, and she was glad they found me. I've never been so sure of God's love before—this moment changed my life.

Melissa, Atlanta, Georgia

The Man in the Tent

In the summer of 2008, I met a man named Jimmy at The Lamb Center, a local day shelter for homeless and poor individuals. I was visiting the center with a group of middle school students as part of a mission week at our church. As the students served food and worked in the laundry, I visited with two of the guests, Jimmy and his wife, Sharon. As we talked, I discovered Jimmy was a student of Scripture and loved to talk about Jesus. He told me the story of how he became homeless and spoke eloquently of the freedom, redemption and healing he had experienced in the years since "Jesus found him." He told me his story with not one ounce of self-pity and gave God all the glory for the changes in his life. He shared how God used The Lamb Center and others he met along his journey to help his wife and him. He also related the ways he was now trying to give back, in whatever way he could, to others in similar circumstances.

One of the most compelling parts of our conversation that day was Jimmy's enthusiastic gratitude for a recent improvement in his living situation. Jimmy and Sharon each told me excitedly that God was providing for them "abundantly" with their recent acquisition of a new tent that didn't leak when it rained. They saw the new tent as clear evidence that God loved them and was providing for their every need, just as Scripture had promised them. For them, a beautiful new tent was all the proof they needed that God and His people saw them, cared about them and wanted to bless them. At the end of the day, I signed up to be a regular volunteer.

I learned about living with a joyful heart of gratitude from a man who lived in a tent.

Kelly, Fairfax, Virginia

The Church

In 2012, it had been six years since I stepped foot in a church. God and I had developed an understanding; He could have my heart, but His congregation was not for me. Too many judging eyes. Too many whispering opinions. Too much heart-break. I was raised in a Christian home, but after a divorce and four years of single motherhood, I felt that scarlet letter burning in my chest every time I entered into the presence of "church folk." So here I was one Sunday morning, newly dating this super great guy. God had his heart, and he was quickly winning mine. But go to church with him? I wanted to say no, but couldn't pass up the opportunity to spend time with him. He played guitar with the worship team, so I decided to go just to watch and listen. I would keep my head down and try to blend in. But blend in, I did not.

Walking into church that morning, with heels too high and a dress too short, thoughts of insecurity crept in. What was I even doing here? What kind of church was this anyway? What if they were ultra conservative, and I walked in there like THIS? I was suddenly and irrevocably convinced I was going to hell. Inner monologue running wild, I grasped tightly to his hand as we walked down the empty hallway. We were early for the service since he was there to practice. Suddenly wondering if I was going to cause him embarrassment, I leaned toward his ear and said, "I think my dress is too short." Before he could even respond to me, a woman suddenly turned the corner in the hallway ahead of us. She reached out her hand to touch my shoulder and without a moment's hesitation said to me, "Sweetie, you look beautiful. Just be yourself." Wow. WOW! That was all I needed.

More than five years later, we attend this church as a family. God has always had my heart, but this church was now my home. In fact, after we got married, we moved 45 minutes north just to be closer to it. The church drew us in. Not with programs or preaching, but with a gentle touch and a few kind words of acceptance from a stranger. I still don't know who that woman was. Chances are I see her every week, but I can't recall her face. Not only did she welcome me, but she challenged me to welcome others in the same way. I try not to walk by an unfamiliar face without offering a smile, a gentle touch, and a few kind words; for I know what such a thing can do.

Cherri, Bella Vista, Arkansas

The Flat Tire

My 3-year-old son and I were driving on the freeway coming home from a camping trip when I blew a tire. This was before cell phones, so I wasn't sure what to do since I had just passed the only freeway exit in sight. I remembered seeing a Denny's on the highway a few minutes back, so I decided my only choice was to backtrack on foot in the hopes of borrowing a phone. Since it was the freeway, I carried my son in my arms.

A few minutes into my walk, a car pulled up and the couple inside offered to help. The gentleman was in a suit and his wife was in her Sunday best. He said he knew it was going to be a dirty job, so he asked if it was okay if he raced home to change. I was terrified for our safety but didn't know what to do. His wife assured me they could help. So I loaded my son into their car. True to his word, we drove down the road to his house where he changed into appropriate clothing. There was a Bible in the man's car. It comforted me. His wife waited in the car with us. Before I knew it, we were back in my car, tire fixed and safe. I never saw them again but so often think of what could have happened to my son and me had God not put them in my path.

Stephanie, Anaheim, California

Angels

My grandmother used to tell the story of why she believed in angels. After my grandfather had his stroke, they struggled to do daily chores. One day, when leaving the grocery store, my grandmother was having quite a time getting her husband back into the car. Suddenly, a young woman came to help them and get my grandfather settled in—no small feat! The way my grandmother used to tell it, she turned around to say thank you to the woman, but she was gone. Poof! Nowhere to be seen. My grandmother believed she had seen an angel that day, one who showed up at just the right time. That young woman, whether angel or human, strengthened my grandmother's faith that God knew their daily trials and would see them through. Supernatural or not, I often think of this story when I see someone struggle. Just a hand, an offer to help, or momentary kind word is enough humanity to sustain a person for another day.

Nicole, Mount Pleasant, South Carolina

The Note

It was an ordinary Sunday morning. I stood in church worshipping with my husband and daughter. We harmonized words that offered praise to God for His goodness, His power and His merciful redemption. A woman sitting a few seats down from me captured my peripheral vision. I suppose my heart was keenly in tune to the movement her tissue-laden hand made as she gently dabbed her liquid pain. Through quivering lips, she formed words to the songs in a brave attempt to hold her world together, but her world seemed to be rolling down her cheeks one teardrop at a time. That morning, my heart was with her. I continued singing and thanked my good, powerful and redeeming God that it wasn't me wiping tears this time.

A few years back, my heart was wounded beyond what I could ever have imagined. The tears flowed and flowed in what felt like a never-ending stream. On an ordinary Sunday morning at church my friend Jana sat beside me. I wasn't aware that my face so clearly told of my pain, but I suppose there was no hiding it. She slipped me a small, folded piece of paper that she had torn from the corner of her notebook. Not daring to read that note at that moment, I tucked it away for later. If the tears started, they might never stop. She had simply written on it, something to the effect of, "I know what the look on your face means. I hope I'm wrong." Jana was keenly aware of what a wounded heart looked and felt like. It was unfortunate that she knew my pain, but she used her experience for my good. Jana gave me an extraordinary gift that day—the gift of being seen, of being known and acknowledged. She gave me the gift of being loved at a time when love was desperately needed. Her little note on the torn off corner of a piece of paper was the hope my soul needed that day.

Years later, on that ordinary Sunday when my eyes caught the tear-filled eyes of another, my heart was stirred. I wanted to connect with her in a tangible way as Jana had done for me. However, I felt God prompting me to pray for her and let Him take care of the rest. So I did. I prayed that she would sense His hope in her hopeless places. I prayed that with each falling tear, the space that it opened would be filled with God's light. I prayed that she would not feel alone in her pain. Jana showed me that we should never underestimate the extraordinary gift we can give with an ordinary act.

Andrea, Surrey, United Kingdom

The Waiting

In April of 2009, I was 17 and attending a conference with my youth group in Portland, Oregon. I was a senior in high school, I'd been accepted into Ecola Bible School and on the outside my life was going well. Internally, things were another story. I was struggling to learn who I was and even what I believed in. I was at a crossroads in my life and I didn't even know it. Over the years I had slowly begun suppressing my emotions. Anytime I didn't want to deal with issues in my life I would just shove them to the side as I walked farther and farther away from God. I had let the hurt of past offenses build up in my heart without letting go, so when the speaker started talking about forgiveness, I lost control. I didn't want to forgive the people in my life. Angry, I got up to walk out of the conference. Before I could make it to the door though, the dam on my emotions broke. I collapsed on the back steps, crying. After years of trying to live a double life, being a Christian at church and doing whatever I wanted when I was with my friends, God had caught up with me. I felt like every bad decision I had ever made was sitting on my shoulders. I was crumbling under the weight. I was scared and didn't know how to get out of the hole I had dug myself into.

A woman I'd never seen before came and sat down next to me. She was a youth leader from another church. She'd been outside walking around with her husband and young son, but when she saw me crying she came and sat down beside me. She took the time to wait out my tears and even found me a few tissues to dry my eyes. She sat talking to me, praying with me, and helping me sort out all my emotions. She reminded me that God loves me. That He hadn't turned His back on me even though I'd walked away. He was waiting for me to come back. By the end of the night she and her husband, Ivan, prayed with me as I rededicated my life to Christ. I never saw them again after that conference but because she was willing to take time to talk to me, God used her to change my life that night. She chose to be obedient when God urged her to stop and ask the crying teenager if she was okay. She was willing to wait out the tears and speak God's love into my life. It may not have seemed like much to her, to just be there for me, but to me it meant everything.

Kattarin, Dorena, Oregon

PEOPLE ARE GOOD...

In Frightful Weather

Chain-Smoking Angel

My son woke up with an ear infection, so I had to make an unplanned trek to the emergency room. While there, the city was hit with an unexpected snow storm, the likes of which I couldn't have even imagined. On the way home from the doctor's office, my van got stuck on unplowed, slick roads (I was driving up a hill). There was an accident behind me, so my son and I sat in the middle of the road unable to get traction of any kind. I could not go forward, and I certainly could not go backward. I began waving at cars, encouraging them to drive around me. As the snow fell even harder, a man with a with a cigarette hanging out of his mouth, driving an old, beat-up pick-up truck, skidded to a stop and said, "What's the matter?" I told him I lost traction and couldn't move in either direction. Without a thought, he turned around (on those crazy roads) and towed me to the top of the hill. When we got to the top, he unhitched me and then followed me down the hill to the entrance of my neighborhood "to make sure I made it home." My son and I named him our "chain-smoking angel."

Amy, Boise, Idaho

The Rain

I had just arrived at a golf course on a rainy Thursday afternoon. I play on a college golf team and on this particular day, we were having a qualifying round to see who would earn a spot to travel to the next tournament. I was somewhat prepared for the stormy weather as I was wearing my rain gear and a hat to keep my head and face dry. The only thing that I was missing was an umbrella. I was walking up to the pro shop and a gentleman was putting his clubs in his car, preparing to leave. I said hello to him to be polite and he asked if we were going out to play even though it was pouring rain. When I told him that we were, he replied by asking if I had an umbrella. I informed him that I did not but that I would be okay without one because I had my waterproof pants and jacket. Without hesitation, he grabbed his own golf umbrella out of the trunk of his car. He insisted that I was to take it. I asked him how I would return it to him and after thinking about it, he said to leave it in the pro shop once I was done with my round. He had not even considered how he would get it back; he just gave it to me so that I could stay dry. I used it the whole round. His kind act played a large role in my qualifying to play in the next tournament. This is a big deal to someone who is on a college golf scholarship.

Madison, Chico, California

The Tornado

I was living in a home on a seven-acre plot south of Crescent, Oklahoma, a small town 30 miles north of Oklahoma City. My father had seven cattle in the pasture behind the house, along with a huge barn. But all that changed on May 3, 1999, when Oklahoma experienced an outbreak of tornadoes that killed 44 people and destroyed 300 homes, including many belonging to several of my neighbors. While my home was damaged, it was not destroyed. We did, however, lose our outbuildings, many of our trees, and all seven of the cattle. They had simply vanished. The tornado's track was clear as it left behind a trail of debris. I was standing outside surveying the destruction, and wondering how I would clean up, when several members of my church family drove up in pickups with tools and wheelbarrows and huge coolers of water. I cried. They helped and I cried. We didn't get it all done in one day, but they were there in the beginning when we needed encouragement and a good start.

Joetta, Edmond, Oklahoma

The Flood

In August 2016, an unprecedented "1,000-year flood" devastated our high-elevation, no-flood-zone home and one of our vehicles in Baton Rouge, Louisiana, the week after my husband and I celebrated our first anniversary. Without flood insurance, we were at a loss as to where to begin. But then people started showing up. Our friends and family, our acquaintances from church, and even an online community jumped into action. They gutted our house, they started a fund, they let us stay in their homes. We are still benefiting from kindnesses in ways that feel surreal nearly a year later.

Rebekah, Baton Rouge, Louisiana

The Hurricane

A few years ago, Hurricane Ike tore through my neighborhood north of Houston, Texas, and left a massive tree on the roof of the home I was renting. Not long after the repairs were done, black mold began appearing on the walls, and I had to move on short notice. I was a single, working mom with no family nearby to help and had no idea how to get my things moved out quickly. Any delay in moving was literally harming our health. I needed a miracle, and, oh, how I got one!

My dear friends came to my aid and carried more boxes up three flights of stairs to my new rental than any of us cared to count. There was so much to do that we couldn't possibly finish in one day. I was running out of time to empty the house and had so much more to move. Worse, I had no more vacation days and couldn't afford to take an unpaid day off. A few days before my moving deadline, a friend called to ask for my house keys, both to the moldy home and to the new-to-me condo. She had made arrangements with a men's small group at our church not only to move my things for me *that* afternoon, but also to make as many trips to storage as it took to stow away the things that wouldn't fit in the condo. What a blessing to a broke and exhausted, working mom! Yes, people *are* good. These people? They were awesome!

Kathleen, The Woodlands, Texas

The Snow

The Treasure Valley in Idaho saw its worst winter in many years in 2017. We normally see two to three inches of snow, and it melts within a day or two. This winter was an entirely different experience. After record-breaking snowfall, our city declared a state of emergency. Two of the four city snow plows were down, and tow trucks were backed up for days. This meant getting out of subdivisions was going to be a challenge. We were on our own.

Because I worked out of my home, I was not as deeply affected as those who had to get to their place of work. My job continued uninterrupted as I worked at my computer. But it kept snowing. Our area came to a standstill as even schools were canceled for a total of nine days. After 16 to 20 inches of snow, I finally had to leave the house for an errand. I made it out of the subdivision, but the snow kept falling. As I returned, I knew the roads would be treacherous around our house. I remembered my husband's instructions about driving in snow and ice—keep moving. I knew where there was a path other vehicles had carved out that I could aim for. If I could hit that stretch, I would have enough momentum to carry me across the road to my driveway. As I started to make the turn, a UPS truck drove inside the cleared ruts. I was forced into the deep snow as I had to drive farther before turning. The snow was so deep that I high-centered on the snow—in the middle of the intersection. Forward or reverse, my wheels only spun. No matter what I did, my car didn't budge.

I looked up, and a clean-cut, young man was at my window, helping me open the door. As I got out of my car, I noticed other people trudging through the heavy snow. A quiet, bearded man appeared and began shoveling. Even though I thanked him, he didn't respond. He was too busy digging. I'm not sure how many others were there. They shoveled snow out from under my car and around the wheels. They pushed and rocked the car but couldn't get it to move. Then a lady pulled up in an SUV and offered her help. When she pulled off her gloves and coat, I noticed her colorful tattoos and lovely smile as she lined up behind my car. My husband arrived and took over the wheel for me as the SUV readied to push my car through the snow and ice into some drivable ruts. When my car finally made it to our driveway, almost everyone had disappeared.

It was crazy hard work and completely unselfish. People had jumped right in without a thought for their own comfort. They only wanted to help someone who needed it. They were from different walks of life, yet differences fade into irrelevance during times of hardship. These people were doing the right thing without expectation of thanks or repayment. These people showed kindness.

Kim, Nampa, Idaho

The Fire

Take a three-year drought, add one downed powerline with 30 mile-per-hour winds and you have a recipe for disaster. That's what happened outside of the small, south central Texas town of Columbus one hot Sunday afternoon in September of 2011. Fueled by the unrelenting winds, the fire quickly grew, blazing a path through the parched piney woods. In no time, the local volunteer fire department became overwhelmed by the intensity of the flames and the speed at which they traveled. But firemen are a band of brothers.

Despite the holiday weekend and 100-degree temperatures, members of as many as 25 volunteer fire departments from across the region abandoned their Labor Day plans to assist our local volunteers. As the fire burned into the night, my family, along with many others, were evacuated and a command post was set up at the local car dealership where folks from Columbus and neighboring towns dropped off countless bottles of water and sports drinks, along with food for the firefighters. In fact, there were so many donations that they had to start turning them away.

Before sunrise the next day, my husband and I returned to check our property, which luckily had been spared. But the image that forever will be seared into my memory is that of a country lane lined with dozens of soot-faced, exhausted firemen lying on their backs, using their helmets as pillows as they tried to catch a few moments of much-needed rest. They didn't have to be there, but they chose to help anyway. "Greater love hath no man than this; that he lay down his life for his friends." (John 15:13, King James Version) These men, strangers to most, were ready to lay down their lives. And the entire community will be forever grateful.

Mindy, Columbia, Texas

PEOPLE ARE GOOD...

When Money Is Tight

Cold Feet

I was 18 years old and had been accepted to a wonderful writing school about an hour outside of Los Angeles. I chose a college near my grandparents as we were very close and I couldn't imagine not being able to hang out with them as I had throughout my life. The first weekend there, my grandpa and aunt came to visit. My grandpa walked into my dorm room to inspect the scene. After looking around a minute or two, the first thing he said was, "Where the hell are your socks? Don't you have any socks?" Indeed, I had no socks. He didn't ask me about my dorm, about the program, about my new friendships. He knew how poor I was and that school loans and scholarships would be the only way I could pay for a school like this. But the sock situation was more than he could handle. Could I really not afford a single pair of socks?

He turned to my aunt and said, "Take off your socks and give them to her." She was dumbfounded. Had her father really just ordered her to remove her own socks? Without another thought, she took off her white bootie socks with the pom poms in the back and handed them to me. I wore them for four years until they were threadbare. My grandpa loved seeing me in those socks. He didn't have a ton of money himself, but there was no way he was going to allow his granddaughter to have cold feet.

Anna, Malibu, California

The Makeup Counter

We had been going through a tough time financially and money had been tight for a while. We'd become adept about modifying our lifestyle so that we spent money only on the necessities. My favorite makeup was not a necessity, so I'd gone more than a year without buying the foundation I love. I received money for my birthday, and I was determined to get my Clinique foundation. I'd been substituting some from the Dollar Store, but it just wasn't the same.

I was very excited to even approach the Clinique counter at the mall. As I rounded the corner, I saw many lovely beauty products, but I was singularly focused on getting my foundation. I felt happy even just being there.

As I started looking for the makeup, an associate came to help me. Her Clinique name badge said she was Olivia. I am not sure if I looked weary or was just unusually quiet, but she asked me lots of questions. I answered. She said to me, "You seem like the kind of person who is always doing for others."

I thought that was a rather strange thing to say, but she must have read on my face that times were tough. I do love to do things for others, but our financial struggles limited what I was able to do. It was as though she had some sixth sense about my situation.

In just a few moments, I discovered it was my time to be on the receiving end of someone's generosity. She retrieved my requested foundation and slipped it into a bag. As she began to ring it up she offered a few more questions. Did I like lipstick? Did I need mascara? Did I like the perfume, Happy? On and on. Every now and then, I would see her bend behind the counter and peek around at me.

When I paid for my foundation, she handed me my bag. It clearly held much more than foundation. It was an entire bag of Clinique samples! Alongside the goodies was a sweet note telling me to come back and see her for a free makeover. On the Happy perfume box, she wrote a simple note that read: "You are AWESOME! From Olivia."

That day, my weary heart really needed a lift, and Olivia's lavish kindness went right down to the depths of my soul. She was a listener who had perceived where I was in life. As I walked out of the store, I had tears in my eyes. God knew exactly what I needed, which wasn't makeup but an empathizing, generous soul to pour into my life.

I will never forget the unusual gift nor the extraordinary girl named Olivia who gave it at just the right moment.

Jeane, Welch, Oklahoma

The Student Loan Payment

I had signed up to spend a year as a volunteer English teacher in a third world country in South East Asia. To do so, I had to raise a decent amount of money (around $15,000 or so) in charitable, tax deductible donations to cover the basic costs (travel, lodging, training and food for the entire year).

As a recent college graduate I also had to figure out how to continue to make payments on my student loans, which at $250 a month, was no small feat. My family was not wealthy by any stretch and neither was I. I gave a short presentation at my dad's church outlining what I would be doing and my financial needs, asking that people understand the need I was trying to meet and invite them to support my efforts financially.

A gentleman that I didn't really know approached me afterwards and said he wanted to pay my student loan payment while I was gone. This was stunning, as I wasn't close to meeting my other financial commitment (which would have been a tax write off for him). Instead this virtual stranger, for over a year, paid $250 a month, faithfully and on time, directly to my bank with no benefit to himself. He had no expectation for anything in return and I never heard from him again. I was able to do the work I was called to do through the kindness of a stranger who expected nothing in return.

Liz, Azusa, California

195

The $5 Bill

My mother was a single parent of five children. She did her best and always worked hard, but ends understandably were often left unmet no matter how hard she tried or how many graveyard shifts she worked. I was in high school and, for years, spent much of my time at my best friend's home. Her parents treated me as their own and repeatedly picked up the slack both in the necessities department as well as in areas that were solely for fun.

One day, a group of kids belonging to a social club in town were all going ice skating. It was planned on a day where most everyone could attend, and it cost $5. I knew there would be no way I could ask my mom for that much money so didn't plan to attend, even though I would be the only one staying home. Everyone gathered at my best friend's home to travel to the event together. I said good-bye and started my trek home. I was about three driveways away when I heard my friend's dad, Paul, calling out to me. He handed me a crumpled $5 bill and said there was no way he was going to let me miss this event.

"These are great girls," he said, "and it would be more fun for everyone if you were there."

I felt elated. He and his wife, Kay, had done so much for me over the years. Their generosity felt endless. To them, it was $5. To me that day, it was everything.

Anna, Boise, Idaho

The Check

My sister received her Ph.D. from UCSF. When she finished, she was strapped with thousands of dollars of loans while searching for a hospital looking to hire a specialist in Neuroendocrinology. She was also proficient in genetics, anatomy, physiology and many other areas of science. Because of her unique skills and loving disposition, she found a job quickly. But just as quickly, she discovered it was not a career that she could imagine doing for a lifetime. Teaching was her passion. When an opportunity came for her to teach part-time at a local junior college, she talked with the lab where she was working full-time and was told she could switch to part-time so that she could follow her passion. This dropped her income significantly with student loans still looming.

Around this time, we were talking on the phone and both agreed that we should get together. We'd been apart for too long! She invited me to visit her, which meant a plane ticket. At the time, I also was struggling financially and said that I would love to visit and would start to save money to make it happen. A few days later I received a card from her with a check for $600. The note inside said, "This is not to pay for a flight to visit me. It is to use however you need to use it. We will see each other again." We both were struggling, and yet she found a way to reach into her own pocket so that sisters could be reunited.

Susan, Battle Lake, Minnesota

The Gift Card

For many years, my husband owned his own construction business and made a good living for our family. Around 2007 and 2008, the market took its huge crash, and everyone stopped building. Work was scarce and before we knew it, we were scraping by. We hadn't really shared our struggles with others, but everyone in our country understood the hard times the industry was facing. For us personally, the situation felt more and more bleak as the months dragged on.

One day we received a card from an anonymous person. Inside was a grocery gift card. What a gift! We were able to purchase food for our family when we really weren't sure how we were going to. It has taught me to be observant to those around us, to recognize when things might be hard so we, too, can help someone just in time.

Hannah, Redding, California

Nita

One Friday morning in 2015, I was out walking my dogs when my husband met me out on the street to tell me that he'd been laid off. With the feeling of fear and uncertainty flooding through me, I left for Bible study shortly thereafter. After hearing the lesson, we all broke into our small groups. At the end of our group time, our Bible study leader asked if we had any prayer requests. I said, "Well, my husband got laid off this morning and I am trying really hard not to freak out."

The women in the group that day showered their love and prayers over me and the situation. One woman in particular, an older lady named Nita, gave me a big hug and pressed some money into my hand. I am not one who takes handouts easily and I felt uncomfortable and completely undeserving. I tried giving it back to her but she refused. I put the money in the pocket of my Bible study folder and told myself that this money would only be used in an emergency. I would not waste this gift. Within a few months, my husband found a new job and Nita passed away with stomach cancer. As for the money, it still sits in the pocket of my Bible study folder where it will be passed on to someone in need—in Nita's honor.

Anita, Redding, California

PEOPLE ARE GOOD...

When Times Are Hard

The Dream Home

My husband and I built our dream home in the beautiful Boise, Idaho, foothills. The views of the sunrises and
sunsets are not only spectacular, but different each day and
night. With my husband soon retiring, we made many plans
for travel and adventure. One week after my husband's retire-
ment, we learned that our home erroneously had been built on
a pre-existing landslide. We were beginning to experience the
shifting of the hill with obvious cracks and movement. No one
was held responsible. We abandoned our dream home once the
utilities were no longer functional.

One morning, knowing that I would need to clear out my
personal belongings as soon as possible, my dear Bible Study
group of nine years arrived on my doorstep. They came with
boxes and scissors and tape and markers, and began lovingly
packing my things. I was emotionally and physically "stunned"
about the reality of losing our home and could do nothing but
walk from room to room as they worked. The comfort and as-
sistance this group gave me during this very difficult time was
beyond faithful. For me, this was a true example of how God
provides for me in challenging situations by bringing others
to my side to walk along with me. We moved on and resettled
and have continued to be blessed with a builder who is willing

to salvage our cabinetry, light fixtures and carpet in order to re-build on solid ground. My husband is no longer retired. Travel and adventure are not in our near future plans, but we have our health and continued grace from our friends for which to give thanks.

Becky, Meridian, Idaho

The Stranger

I had given birth to my second child and was overjoyed with the idea of flying my 6-week-old daughter and my 2-year-old son to my childhood home to meet my parents. They lived in Canada so the flight from my home required a stopover in Seattle. My husband could have joined us had I been willing to wait for him to get a few days off, but I was too excited for that. I had made this flight with my son many times, so didn't think it would be a big deal. Who knew that two planes were, at that moment, flying into the twin towers in an act of terrorism never before seen in the United States.

I landed in Seattle to find the airport in chaos. Even my baby awakened upset and hungry. I quickly raced to the restroom to feed her. I still had no idea what was going on, why there was panic on the faces of those around me. I was so focused on my two kids and our stroller and our carry-ons that I didn't have a second to ask what was happening. I finally finished in the bathroom and was shocked to see people crying and running and making frantic phone calls. What was happening?!

A flight attendant told me all connecting flights were being canceled and that I needed to get my kids out of the airport. But I have to get to Canada, I explained, still not understanding. A stranger looked me in the eye and said I needed to get out of the airport and that he would help me. We went down to baggage claim where hundreds of black bags stuffed the carousels. There was a sea of suitcases. They all looked the same. My baby was crying, my son was becoming more anxious and the only thing I knew was that some planes had crashed into a building on the other side of the U.S. But this stranger knew. He stayed with me until we found my luggage. He then helped me get the kids, the stroller and the bags into a taxi where he was sure we would be safe. He made it his mission to get a mom and her two precious babies out. He gave me strength to handle what the TV would soon explain.

Candace, Canada

Marilee

My prayer partner, Marilee, shared a lesson with me that forever changed the way I saw other people. As the single mom of a daughter with special needs, I was stubbornly independent, determined to make a go of it on my own. But after my daughter had surgery in April 1994, I struggled to balance work and caring for her. Money was tight, and I was so exhausted that I spent most days in a fog. Things like my own food and housework took a low priority. Then one night, my prayer partner showed up at my door with supper, a big container of stir-fried chicken. I was thrilled, surprised . . . and embarrassed. I had been in my new church less than a year, but she and I had become fast friends. *Did she really think I couldn't handle this on my own? Did the church think that?*

I thanked her but protested. "I really can do this without help."

She looked at me as if I'd sprouted an extra head. "Of course, you can. I don't doubt that for a moment. But let me ask you this. Do you not get a special blessing from helping other people?"

I didn't even have to think. "Of course, I do."

She nodded. "Then why are you trying to deny me my blessing? Most people truly enjoy helping others. Good people really do want to help out. Now hush and eat."

And with that, she set to cleaning up my apartment. She was right. Later, other members of the church fell in line behind her, helping me with this and that. Her words became a permanent part of the way I view people. Most people really do enjoy helping others. Social media and news reports are full of instances when strangers come together to lift a car off a trapped person, or group together to save someone from drowning. Sometimes the ills of the world can make us feel jaded and isolated. But, as those words reminded me, most people are good, and more than eager to help each other.

Ramona, Birmingham, Alabama

The Lawn

My family endured an incredibly tough year in 2009. My daughter was diagnosed with trigonocephaly when she was 16 weeks old. The months between the diagnosis and the reconstructive surgery were a source of significant stress. We did a good job finding care for our older son and dogs, and for our house. To say we were on top of things was an understatement; it felt like we had everything covered.

But by August, the bottom was falling out.

We had to change doctors because our original doctor left the practice. Our new neurosurgeon would not work with our "old" reconstructive surgeon, and one of the dogs became ill, rendering our original boarding plan worthless. Then the phone rang; it was my husband. He was rushing his mother to the emergency room and he didn't know if she was going to make it. He spent the next several weeks alternating between All Children's Hospital for our baby and the ICU for his mom and trying to make arrangements for care for his dad.

Outside our house, the grass grew. And grew. And grew. It finally got so high that someone in our neighborhood reported us to county code enforcement. On the same day that my husband's father was admitted to the ICU of a second hospital, we were given 48 hours to get our yard, gutters and so forth cleaned up or we would be fined.

It so happened that our next-door neighbor, Mark, pulled into his driveway as I was standing in the front yard with my 3-year-old, trying to figure out what to do. He came over to find out what was going on, and before I knew what was happening, he had marshaled an army who came to our rescue. Our lawn was cut, our roof cleaned off, our front garden cleaned out, and branches trimmed off the enormous oak tree in the front yard. The next day, the code enforcement officer returned and was amazed at the work accomplished. I explained it would never have been possible without the help of our neighbor. Every two weeks, like clockwork, someone showed up to mow our lawn from that day in August until after Katie's surgery in October. Mark didn't want us to be concerned with the lawn with so many other things happening. It was such a small thing, but one that held enormous value to us.

Elizabeth, Brandon, Illinois

The Plaque

My husband and I met while we were both teachers and coaches at a small private school. Once I was expecting our first child, I left the teaching world behind in order to stay home but continued to mingle as part of the close-knit athletic community. As football season changed to baseball and back again, I often bundled our tiny daughter and headed out for team dinners, games and post-game meals with the other coaches and their wives. I spent a lot of time with these families as we celebrated our sporting successes. During that time, I met Dee, who was also a coach's wife. She had grown boys in high school and I was a new mom with one baby on my hip and another on the way. We had sports and our faith in common, but clearly were in different phases with our children. But that didn't stop her from offering me friendship and hope when I most needed it.

With the arrival of our new baby, we were sent on a journey to find answers as to why our sweet girl was delayed in her growth and development. Months later, in September 1998, I sat in an examination room at Children's Hospital as a geneticist spoke the words that changed our lives forever. Cornelia de Lange Syndrome. Thanks to an extremely rare—and random—mutation of a gene, our little Princess was destined for a different future than the one I had imagined for her. On our way out the door, an intern handed us a few pages of information printed from the internet and I practically memorized the prognosis during the drive home. Soon the words of the doctor and those written on the page blended together into a swirling and confusing mess. Mental retardation. She would "probably" walk and "probably" talk if we got her into physical therapy and speech therapy as soon as possible. Autistic-like behaviors. A future filled with specialists.

Of course, the sun rose the next morning. My husband went back to work and on to football practice while I stayed home with the kids, laundry, and a stack of papers staring at me from the coffee table. My perfectionistic self had struggled to adjust to our new reality. No straight A's for our girl. No college. No prom. No driving. Not to mention the social stigma and her other challenges. It wasn't supposed to be like this. My dreams were swept away in a hurricane of emotion.

That evening, my husband arrived home with a gift bag from Dee. Inside was a small plaque with the picture of a storm-tossed sailboat and these words: "Sometimes God calms the storm and sometimes He lets the storm rage . . . and calms His child." Hope washed over me. It would be okay. Others had promised to pray for us, but Dee gave me a promise to hang onto. Eighteen adventure-filled years later, it still hangs on our wall as a reminder that God is always with me in the middle of the storm.

Candee, Loveland, Colorado

The Spanish Paper

On the second-to-last day of my junior year in college, my worst academic nightmare came true. My laptop, the one that had helped me through almost three years of papers and exams, had an irreparable power failure. With an ominous "Pew!" the screen went blank and nothing in my arsenal of tricks did a thing. After a few hours, even the Geek Squad had pronounced it dead with no definite chance of recovering the data. But I didn't have the time they needed to try. Like it or not, I had to rewrite 12 pages of my Spanish Lit research paper plus the remaining eight AND move out before noon the next day or face a fine. Or worse, risk my A in the class! I don't think I'll ever be able to pick up Isabel Allende's *La Casa de los Espiritus* without feeling that lost time and brain space. But I'll always remember the way my friends packed my dorm room and filled up my car—in the rain, no less—as I feverishly typed in my non-native language. I've never been good at asking for help, and yet there they were. A little before my deadline, I hit send on that paper, closed the lid of my new laptop, and turned in my room keys to find a fully loaded car pulled up to the curb. The see-you-in-August hugs were extra sweet that day in May 2005 with the knowledge that I'd be coming back to a community willing to surround each other in the big and small things, whenever needed.

Laurie, Tulsa, Oklahoma

Her Hand

I lived in New York City on September 11, 2001, and on that day, my perspective of humanity drastically changed. My company dismissed everyone for the day after the attack, but the New Jersey Transit shut down, so there was no way for me to get across the Hudson River to New Jersey where I lived. I was in my early 20s, and alone since I had no family on the east coast. I met up with a friend who lived near me in New Jersey and also worked only a few blocks from me in Manhattan. His cousin lived in lower Manhattan and said we could stay there until the trains started running again. As we walked over 70 blocks toward downtown, we both commented on how different everyone was acting. We witnessed New Yorkers' kindnesses to one another. They seemed to have a sense of silent unity in our circumstance.

After staying with his cousin for a few hours, the New Jersey Transit re-opened. We boarded a bus, which would take us to the New Jersey Path Train. It was almost full so that I couldn't sit next to my friend but I found an empty window seat next to a woman. As the bus drove through downtown and turned onto a different street, I saw the smoke. The terrifying cloud of destruction loomed over the city like a smoke signal to the world. The bus moved along, and I saw a woman standing on a corner with white powder in her hair and on her clothing. She stood alone, looking stunned and forlorn. I wanted badly to help her, to reach through the glass and console her in some way, but the bus moved onward. I felt alone and powerless. I couldn't help that woman. I couldn't help any of them.

Frustration filled me, and I leaned against the window and began to cry silently, my heart aching for that woman, for all those who died, their families and their children. I felt someone taking my hand. It was the woman next to me on the bus, and I looked over at her. She gave me a look that said a thousand things. Without words, she knew how I felt because she felt the same way. Her eyes told me, "You are not alone. We will overcome this." I will never forget how a stranger made me feel like I was amongst close family in such a large city. When we got off the bus, she hugged me, and we went our separate ways without saying a word.

In the wake of a hate-filled act of terror, the city blossomed in love. I saw people treating one another with patience, understanding and kindness. I will never forget how beautiful humanity can be in the midst of terror and destruction.

Audra, Atlanta, Georgia

Watercolors

My mother loved to paint. When I was a little girl, I remember she would take us to open fields where she would set up her easel and paint while we played nearby. Her oil paintings were a treasured collection in my home, growing up and later, once I became an adult with wall space of my own. Life got busy and my mom didn't paint for several years until she was invited to go to Baja to stay at her friend Lynn's house. Lynn expressed an interest in learning to paint with watercolors, so my mom decided to try her hand at painting with watercolors, too. Together they would sit on Lynn's patio and paint the view of the ocean or the sunrise, or the surrounding landscapes. Before she knew it, my mom was heading down to Baja once a year, a new tradition that she cherished.

One year Lynn had the idea to invite a few more friends and hire a watercolor teacher. "It will be a painting retreat!" she said. My mom went to that retreat for several years. When she was diagnosed with pancreatic cancer, my mom decided to have an art show on her front lawn to display all of her oil paintings and many of the watercolors that she had done in Baja. It was a happy day. Lynn came to the art show and assured my family that she would be there for us during the difficult months to come. These were lovely words, but I didn't know her like my mom did so thought they were just that . . . words. True to those words, though, Lynn stayed by my mom's side during the hard days. A few months after my mom passed away, when I was ready, she invited me to join her at the next painting retreat in Baja. I would go in my mom's spot. It was an amazing experience for me to be learning to paint water-colors in a place that my mom loved so much with a group of women who knew and loved my mom.

Kate, Sunnyvale, California

PEOPLE ARE GOOD...

When We Are Consumed by Grief

The Night Nurse

I was pregnant with twins. Thrilled beyond belief. My 10-year-old daughter and 6-year-old son couldn't wait for their baby sisters to arrive.

That morning we had an ultrasound. Both babies looked great! Growing as they should. We were still five weeks from their due date, but had hit the magic week where we knew their lungs would be fully developed if they were born early. I had signed paperwork for a C-section just in case.

By the time I was heading to bed that night, I knew something was happening. I had been uncomfortable for weeks and barely sleeping, but this felt different. Around 2 a.m., I got up because I suddenly had a great urge to charge our video camera. I had just plugged it in when my water broke. This had happened with both my older children so it didn't bother me too much, except it seemed like a lot of blood compared to before. But I was having twins so this was different.

Mom and Dad came over to stay with our other two kids and my husband swept me off to the hospital about 20 minutes away.

Upon arrival I was hooked up to monitors to find each heartbeat. Suddenly the mood shifted in the room. The nurses began frantically calling the doctor and we were informed that they could only find one heartbeat. Excited smiles were quickly replaced with urgent voices. My husband was being sent out of the room just as I was put under for an emergency C-section. The doctor's last question to us was, "If one of them doesn't make it, do you still want your tubes tied?" My husband replied, "Yes." My brain was still trying to grasp what the doctor meant by her question. Of course my babies would be fine. And then I was out.

I awoke to see my husband with my beautiful baby Nicole in his arms. He immediately handed her to me. "Where's Amber?"

He said, "I was told that they were able to get her heart going but all her vital organs were failing."

WHAT ARE YOU SAYING TO ME?

Amber only stayed on Earth for 11 hours. My brother and sister-in-law were allowed to sit in the NICU and hold her as she passed. Having just had a C-section, I wasn't able.

As night approached again, I was going on two days with no sleep. The nurses kept telling me I needed to let Nicole go to the nursery and rest, but there was NO WAY she was leaving my sight. They said the night shift would be coming in soon, so I would meet the nursery nurse. I didn't care! I would never sleep again if that's what it took to ensure my Nicole was safe.

As night stretched on, my exhausted husband left the hospital to care for my devastated older children. Just as the fatigue began to take over, I was approached by the nursery nurse.

A familiar voice said, "Hola, señora, I'm so sorry for your loss."

I'm a high school Spanish teacher. This nurse who came to me like an angel was not only a former student, but one of my favorites. She said so gently and sincerely, "You need to sleep now, but don't worry. I will hold Nicole for you all night. I won't put her down. If she needs to nurse I'll bring her right to you. Whatever your family needs right now, I'm here for you."

This beautiful nurse was there when I needed her most. She kept all those promises not just that night, but all three nights I was in the hospital. I finally could sleep knowing Nicole was safe.

One nurse helped me keep it together. She will forever have a special place with our family.

Elizabeth, Yucaipa, California

The Letter

At work, in June of 1999, I met a lovely woman named Carol. Because of the nature of my job, I have seen her twice a year for the last 18 years. She brought me gourmet cookies every time she came in. We became friends, and we shared all of life's twists and turns. About 10 years ago, she had to have a kidney transplant, her only remaining kidney having failed. A stranger, who was a match, donated one of hers. Things went well and she was able to get back to doing the things she loved. Then, about a year ago, she told me that she had been struggling with a recurring blood infection but that it was being managed with antibiotics.

We scheduled her next appointment as usual. Last week I received a letter at work from Carol. It was a thank you note, handwritten on a handmade card. It read, "Dear Leslie, I hate to break this news to you . . . but I've been diagnosed with an acute leukemia and don't have much time left. I have really enjoyed our friendship over these last 18 years, and I wish you the very best. With much love, Carol." This card is so precious to me. That Carol took the time to write me a letter, to make her dying easier for me, shows a truly kind and selfless spirit.

Leslie, Boise, Idaho

Empty

It was an eerie feeling, being so detached from a world with billions of people; segregated from those continuing to move through their lives as if their world was untouched by my deep grief. It was as if they couldn't see me. Where were my friends? Where were my family members? My husband came home from work every day and tried to reach me but he couldn't quite break through the dark chasm around my heart. My daughter hugged me. My infant son nestled against my chest. Still the grief overwhelmed me. I needed a ray of hope. Some speck of joy.

It had been four months since my mom had passed at the young age of 43. And still I hurt. My chest held a gaping hole and frequently stole my breath. Rivers of tears came at their leisure. Why couldn't I move past this? She was gone to a better place. A place where she could run and move freely. A place where she could sing with joy and burst with happiness. Heaven. But I was exiled into my own personal hell. A place where no matter how far my hand stretched, it was never quite long enough to make contact. Where was that hope in the Lord I had heard so much about? Why didn't His grace cover me? Why was I left all alone to figure out this mess my life had become? I couldn't do it. I couldn't pretend like I was okay for one more minute. I couldn't go back to the church where I felt brushed aside. So I stopped. I stopped going to church. I stopped hanging out with friends. I stopped believing that anyone cared. I began to move through my life as an empty shell. I loved my husband and my kids but it still didn't penetrate the ever-present sadness. I was empty.

For six long months I moved through my life on auto-pilot. Until finally someone reached out to me with words that penetrated my darkness. "Perhaps you've never really had the joy and grace of our God. Let's pray for you to receive that now." At last someone saw me. Someone had the answer. Knowing that I needed to hear those words, God sent her to me and she came willingly. Her words broke through and opened my eyes and heart for God to change me forever. I am no longer an empty shell. I no longer am consumed by the darkness or overwhelming grief. My faith in God and the church was restored because someone cared enough to see me.

Brandi, Oxford, Alabama

MOPS

In 2013, when my mother's battle with early onset Alzheimer's disease finally ended, the members of my Mothers of Preschoolers (MOPS) steering team banded together to fill, and deliver to my house, a gigantic laundry basket full of snacks, paper plates, plastic silverware, napkins and restaurant and grocery store gift cards. At the time, I had no idea how desperately I would need those items as the busy days after my mother's death filled with funeral planning turned into long days filled with grief and mental, physical and emotional exhaustion. The thoughtfulness of those MOPS mommas gave me, a young, tired and somewhat distraught mother, the energy to keep going (and the blessing of not needing to wash dishes for weeks)!

Lauren, Buda, Texas

People Are Good...

During the Holidays

The Tree

In July of 2001, my family endured a terrible tragedy that claimed the life of my 4-year-old daughter, Teagan. We were enjoying Sunday brunch when a suicidal woman drove her car into the restaurant where we sat. We were the first table hit. There were weeks of ICU for all of my family members due to critical injuries and months of rehab. Added to this, of course, was the grief and sorrow that filled our hearts and lives.

As the holidays grew closer that year, we were so broken-hearted we didn't know what to do with our pain. Jingly music, decorations and lights seemed to mock us rather than bring any sense of joy. As I wept and questioned how to survive the season, a friend of ours suggested to me that I decorate and donate a tree in memory of my daughter to a local charity auction coming up. I decided I would create "Teagan's Dream Tree" and cover the tree with things she loved, including pink and purple shiny bulbs, shimmery ribbon and even a Barbie doll angel on top. It was a labor of love and I cried the whole time I set the tree up, but when it was finished I could almost picture Teagan beaming at it from Heaven.

The night of the auction event came and my husband and I mustered strength and dressed up to attend the occasion. We knew it would be hard but we were grateful to be able to give back to a great cause in our daughter's memory. The evening was festive and Teagan's tree was auctioned off last—the event coordinators called it "the belle of the ball." It took top dollar.

We cried but also felt a bit of joy realizing that pushing through our grief had brought benefit and goodness to someone else. It was the following morning that surprised us and helped us see even more clearly that even giving out of sorrow had its reward. The gentleman who had won Teagan's dream tree with his top-dollar bid had the tree delivered and set up in our home. He said it was right and fitting that the tree should be given back to us as it held such meaning, and he wanted our family to know the whole community continued to care deeply for our sorrow-filled hearts. We hadn't planned to get a tree that year. It would have been too hard. Instead, though, we were given not only a fully-decorated, sentimental tree, but a gift of having our burdens shared. We were offered a glimpse that the world still held so much beauty, goodness, kindness and even joy in the midst of deep grief and sorrow. For so many reasons, it was a Christmas we never will forget.

Jody, location unknown

Tinsel

In February of 2013, my dad passed away. It was devastating for me as he and I had always been close. In the fall of that same year, in my driveway I met Rose, the mother of my new neighbor. We started talking about our parents and I told her that I had lost my dad earlier that year and was not looking forward to a Christmas without him. I LOVE Christmas and all the traditions that come with it as I was fortunate and grateful to be raised by "Mr. and Mrs. Christmas." Every year I put tinsel on our live, real tree, something my dad always did. I was telling Rose that I didn't have much tinsel left and stores didn't stock it as it apparently no longer was the "in" thing. So after Christmas that year, Rose had seen a couple boxes of tinsel in some random store and she bought it for me. Then Christmas two years later there were six boxes of tinsel by my front door! I was so emotional and grateful for this gesture. To think that Rose not only remembered my heartbreak, she also took the time to help me get through Christmas without my dad. She helped keep my special tradition alive!

Cathy, Boise, Idaho

Raggedy Ann

One of the greatest gifts of love and kindness that I have ever received came to me one Christmas morning when I was just a child. On this particular Christmas day, under the Christmas tree sat a beautiful Raggedy Ann doll. This was no ordinary Raggedy Ann doll as she had not been purchased in a store. This doll was stitched together by my mother's own hands. My mom, a single parent to five young children, worked the graveyard shift as a nurse in a hospital to make ends meet and provide for her children. My mom gave me a gift that no amount of money could ever buy. She gave me the gift of love. And, this Christmas morning, her gift of love was in the shape of this Raggedy Ann doll.

I don't know how my mom found time to make this doll for me as she worked all night long and cared for five children during the day. I don't know where she learned the skills needed to make the doll. I don't even know how she paid for the materials. What I do know is that when I look at that doll, I see so much more than red yarn hair or triangle-shaped eyes. I see far past the little apron that has my name stitched on it. What I see is my mom and her love woven into every stitch. Forty years later, that Raggedy Ann doll is still with me. Her

face is now tear stained and her clothes have lost their bright-
ness, but the love that my mom worked into her remains. It
remains in her and it remains in me.

Nini, Redlands, California

The Wallet

In December 2011, I was traveling from Los Angeles back to my home in Michigan. I had a traveling job that kept me on the road 40 or more weeks out of the year. I was at the busy LAX airport during Christmastime where I was purchasing some snack items. The cash register at the gift shop wasn't working for one reason or another, so the clerk asked if I wouldn't mind paying at a different register. I moved my items, grabbed my credit card and went on my way. I did not realize I had left my wallet sitting by the original cash register. I hurried onto the plane at the end of the terminal when my phone rang. I still had not realized that I was without my wallet. I answered the phone and spoke to a manager at a Walgreens who told me that someone had found my wallet, found this business card for Walgreens in my wallet and called and asked if I would be alright if they passed my information along so they could return my wallet.

The door was closing on the plane, so of course I said, "Yes, please, absolutely!" I gave the manager my address and had to hang up the phone quickly as airplanes don't like to wait. I didn't know what to expect, but I was grateful someone had my wallet.

I arrived back to my home in Michigan that night, and the next day FedEx came to my house. Overnighted, express delivery, was not only my wallet, but a NEW wallet with a note. It said, "It looks like you could use a new wallet since this one has seen some miles. Please accept this Christmas gift and pay it forward. May God bless you in your travels. Merry Christmas! Linda." My wallet had all the original contents, the $100 cash, and no way to contact this amazing person. Linda probably spent $80 or more overnighting this package to me, plus the cost of a very nice new wallet. She was truly an angel sent to help that day. I remember sitting in my stairway in utter shock that this had all transpired. It absolutely renewed my faith in human kindness.

Lucas, Boise, Idaho

The Christmas Carols

A year and a half ago, I was diagnosed with multiple myeloma (incurable bone/marrow cancer), and following a year of twice-weekly chemo and a stem cell transplant, I was housebound, with no immune system to protect me from contaminants. There was no choice but to cancel our traditional big-table-lotsa-family Thanksgiving AND the 30-plus people at a sit-down Christmas dinner.

To say I felt down about not spending the holidays with the grandorables is an understatement. Then, on Christmas night, 2016, my husband called me onto our sun porch. Exhausted (and feeling pretty sorry for myself), I slumped out there . . . and saw our kids and grandkids gathered in a semi-circle on the deck. A glowing blaze in the fire pit backlit them; on tables beside them, hot chocolate in Styrofoam cups; in their hands, lyrics to half a dozen classic Christmas carols. With windows to protect me from any school-related germs, they sang . . . and so did my heart. It was by far the best and most memorable gift I'd ever received. Whose idea was this glorious Christmas treasure? My loving husband, of course!

Loree, Baltimore, Maryland

The Rescue

It was my first major holiday away from home. I knew I wouldn't be able to go home so I volunteered to work that morning. All my roommates were going out of town for Thanksgiving, and after work I planned to spend a lonely afternoon at home. When one of my roommate's parents found out, they invited me to come to their home to enjoy dinner with all of their extended family instead. Once work was over I headed out.

It was a beautiful day with leaves falling from the tall trees. Unfamiliar with the winding road, I drove along just a bit under the speed limit. A car came flying up behind me. As it edged closer and closer, I tried to speed up but it wouldn't back off, staying right on my bumper. With relief I spotted a passing lane just ahead. I slowed down a bit, hoping the driver would get the hint, but he ignored the opportunity to go around me and came even closer. I was getting scared and in a moment of panic I decided to pull over, not realizing just how narrow the shoulder of the road was. Instead of moving to the other lane to pass me, he stayed right where he was. I jerked my wheel to get out the way, sending both of my passenger side tires off the edge of the road as the stranger sped out of sight. My car was now parked precariously, partially off the road and slanting toward a steep ditch. I wasn't sure if I should try to get out and risk shifting the car, possibly causing it to fall, or just stay where I was, hoping it didn't roll with me inside.

Finally gaining the courage to climb out, I discovered that although the car was stuck, it was not in danger of immediately flipping over. Now I was left standing on the side of the road with no one to call for help. My family was in another state, my roommates were out of town and I didn't have a phone number for the friends I was going to see. All I could do was pray for help. Several people stopped but no one had the means to help, that is, until a family on the way home came to my rescue. The dad and teenage son went home to get their truck and tow chain, while the mom and teenage daughter stayed to talk with me and keep me calm as I prayed they would be able to get me out of this mess. When they returned, they hooked up my car and pulled me back on to the road without a problem. To them it was just a simple matter of stopping to help some girl on Thanksgiving. To me it was a rescue and the answer to my Thanksgiving Day prayer.

Kattarin, Dorena, Oregon

Thanksgiving Dinner

I grew up with six siblings—I was stuck in the middle—and a hardworking, single mom. She was a full-time nurse but still struggled to make ends meet. She was talented in so many ways so did several side jobs to help bring in extra money. One of those jobs was selling flowers via roadside. We older kids would set up our stands and sell flower arrangements on holidays. I can remember one Thanksgiving being out in the cold. A man stopped to buy flowers, nothing out of the ordinary. But about 30 minutes later he returned with a huge warm plate of Thanksgiving fixings. I was famished and completely overwhelmed both by his thoughtfulness and by the idea that he had noticed me alone—and hungry. That one Thanksgiving gesture changed the way I look at people and challenged me to pay forward the generosity shared that day.

Jonathan, Redding, California

Valentine's Day

I was sitting in a local coffee shop and I was in a bad mood. It was crowded and loud and I had a lot of work to do on my computer. I often escaped to this location when I needed to think and was frustrated that so many people thought to do the same that day. Even though it was early, the line for coffee stretched all the way to the door. It took me 15 minutes to get my drink. I didn't think the day could get worse until a familiar woman floated in the door. She was a regular like me but I did not know her. I say floated because she was happy and had a message to share with each of us, "Happy Valentine's Day!" she shouted. I found myself thinking *Lady, nobody cares about Valentine's Day. Pipe down.* But she was determined. She went from customer to customer wishing each a Happy Valentine's Day. After a few minutes of this, a noticeable difference circulated. People seemed cheerful and delighted. The owner noticed as well and was grateful for the change. He offered each of us a free cup of coffee to celebrate the day. I admit it. I felt the change, too. Not just because of the free coffee, but because someone was interested in sharing a little bit of joy, no matter what some of us were thinking. A stranger with a simple message turned the day around for me and, I am guessing, a room full of others.

Anonymous

NOTES

1. Laetitia Mizero Hellerud, West Fargo, North Dakota (originally from Burundi), author of *Being at Home in the World: Cross-Cultural Leadership Lessons to Guide Your Journey.*

2. Dr. Susan Vitalis' *Still Listening: How to Hear God's Direction at Life's Crossroads.*

ACKNOWLEDGMENTS

This book would not be possible without the selfless contributions of our storytellers. With hundreds of submissions, we had the beautiful challenge of choosing stories that would connect with our readers on a variety of levels. We also were blessed to be working with some of the best designers, editors and writers around.

We'd like to share a special thanks with our publisher, Maryanna Young, of Aloha Publishing, as well as those people on her team who were deeply committed to the project, including Dave Troesh, Melissa Lambert, Mindy Hubbard, Jen Regner and Amy Hoppock. We also thank Jeane Wynn for the heart and friendship she brought to this project, both in story collection as well as sharing the work. Thank you Gina Cafiero for your unmatched photography and Leslie Hertling for turning her work into an unforgettable cover. Thank you also to Fusion Creative Works for creating a memorable design for our book. We are grateful to each of you for your willingness to share your gifts with us.

Mostly, though, we would like to thank our family who not only contributed their own stories to our collection, but also afforded us the time to pursue a project that we believe will be a tiny contribution toward making the world a more joy-filled, hopeful place. Thank you Mike, Elena, Giacomo and Gabriella McHargue, and thank you Mark, Madison, Markie and Tanner Stephens. You are our everything.

Heartfelt thanks to our Papa, Louis Runfola, for his willingness to love and to see the good in people, always. Lastly, of course, thanks to our beloved Jesus, for His continual presence.

Anna McHargue and Anita Stephens,
Words With Sisters

Our Contributors:

Amy Hoppock

Andrea Stunz

Angela Lovenburg

Angie Dailey

Audra York

Audrey Smith

Becky Rowan

Beth Hines

Beth Walker

Betsy Miller

Brandi O'Brien

Brian Smith

Candace Gibson

Candee Fick

Cara Grandle

Cara Osborne

Cara Putnam

Cassie Nations

Cathy Ruim

Charissa Plymesser

Cherri Rodriguez

Christine Schichtle

Crystal Joy

Curt Harding

Cynthia Roemer

Dave Savage

Dave Troesh

Deb Murray

Deena Peterson

Elena McHargue

Elisa Cleary

Elise Slattery

Elizabeth Calbreath

Elizabeth Latshaw-Foti

Gabriella McHargue

Gina Marie Cafiero

Hannah Howell

Heather Snyder

Jeane Wynn

Jennifer Gentry

Jessica Guest

Jessica Gaylord

Jessica Wiggins

Jody Ferlaak

Joetta Beauchene

Jonathan Howell

Josh Cranfill

June Covington

Kate Chapman

Kathleen Turner

Kattarin Kirk

Katy Epling

Kelly Johnson

Kelly Smith

Kent Kalpakjian

Kimberly Kalpakjian

Kim Foster

Kim Sutherlin Cook

Kim Thuleen

Kira Lunde

Krissy Cabot

Krista Wilbur

Laetitia Mizero Hellerud

Larry W. Timm

Lauren Flake

Laurie Tomlinson

Leslie Hertling

Leslie Mattson

Lindsay Hufford

Lisa Aggarwal

Liz McHargue

Liz VanSkike

Loree Lough

Lorraine Kerr

Louis Runfola

Lucus Kevan

Madison Stephens

Mark Stephens, Jr.

Mark Traylor

Mary Molina

Maryanna Young

Meg Forest

Melissa Lambert

Michele Barbera

Michael McHargue

Mindy Obenhaus

Nicole Seitz

Nini Stephens

Peter Leavell

Ramona Richards

Rebekah Johnson Maricelli

Robin Dauma

Rosalie Barber

Roy Aggarwal

Savanna Kaiser

Stacey

Stacey Stone

Stephanie Clinton

Stephanie Troesh

Stephannie Hughes

Susan Vitalis

Tanner Stephens

Tara Royer Steele

Tisha Purdy

Vicki Hirth

Vincent Runfola

If you have a story that you would like considered for our next publication, please visit www.wordswithsisters.com/people-are-good and complete the Submission Criteria form.

ABOUT THE AUTHOR

AnnaMarie McHargue has been a book editor for over 30 years. Her passion for beautiful words is something she loves to share with the reading public. She and her sister, Anita Stephens, co-founded their company, Words With Sisters, with the mission of partnering with authors who wish to offer positive messages and inspiration through their work.

Anna lives in Boise, Idaho, with her husband, Mike, their three children, Elena, Jack and Gabriella, and their bulldog, Vince.

56800414R00163

Made in the USA
San Bernardino, CA
14 November 2017